T0192418

Beginning Cloud Native Development with MicroProfile, Jakarta EE, and Kubernetes

Java DevOps for Building and Deploying Microservices-based Applications

Tarun Telang

Apress®

Beginning Cloud Native Development with MicroProfile, Jakarta EE, and Kubernetes: Java DevOps for Building and Deploying Microservices-based Applications

Tarun Telang
Hyderabad, India

ISBN-13 (pbk): 978-1-4842-8831-3   ISBN-13 (electronic): 978-1-4842-8832-0
https://doi.org/10.1007/978-1-4842-8832-0

Managing Director, Apress Media LLC: Welmoed Spahr
Acquisitions Editor: Steve Anglin
Development Editor: Laura Berendson
Coordinating Editor: Gryffin Winkler
Copy Editor: Kezia Endsley

Cover designed by eStudioCalamar

Cover image by Pixabay (www.pixabay.com)

Distributed to the book trade worldwide by Apress Media, LLC, 1 New York Plaza, New York, NY 10004, U.S.A. Phone 1-800-SPRINGER, fax (201) 348-4505, e-mail orders-ny@springer-sbm.com, or visit www.springeronline.com. Apress Media, LLC is a California LLC and the sole member (owner) is Springer Science + Business Media Finance Inc (SSBM Finance Inc). SSBM Finance Inc is a **Delaware** corporation.

For information on translations, please e-mail booktranslations@springernature.com; for reprint, paperback, or audio rights, please e-mail bookpermissions@springernature.com.

Apress titles may be purchased in bulk for academic, corporate, or promotional use. eBook versions and licenses are also available for most titles. For more information, reference our Print and eBook Bulk Sales web page at http://www.apress.com/bulk-sales.

Any source code or other supplementary material referenced by the author in this book is available to readers on GitHub (https://github.com/Apress). For more detailed information, please visit http://www.apress.com/source-code.

Printed on acid-free paper

This book is dedicated to my grandparents, parents, wife Nikita, and son Vihan. They have always been a source of inspiration and encouragement to me. It's also for all of the software and technology creators who work hard to make our planet a better place to live.

—Tarun Telang

Table of Contents

About the Author

Tarun Telang is a hands-on technologist with extensive experience in the design and implementation of multitiered, highly scalable software applications. He has been part of several well-known companies, including Microsoft, Oracle, Polycom, and SAP. He has over 17 years of experience in architecting and developing business applications.

He began his career as an enterprise Java developer at SAP, where he developed distributed application software for big firms. He got his start with enterprise session beans and message-driven beans, as well as instrumenting enterprise applications' configuration and management using the Java Management Extensions (JMX) technology.

He quickly mastered various enterprise technologies, including the Enterprise Beans, Java Management Extensions, Servlets, and Server Pages technologies, and in his first year as a developer, he became a Sun Certified Programmer for the Java Platform, Standard Edition 6, and an SAP Certified Development Consultant for the SAP NetWeaver Java Web Application Server (which was a Java EE 5-compliant application server).

He also gained expertise in XML technologies like XSLT and XSD. He developed several solutions using session beans and message-driven beans to handle message-oriented communications across numerous systems. In 2007, Tarun was named an SAP Mentor and Community Influencer for his articles and blog posts on emerging technologies and for promoting innovative solutions in the SAP Developer Community. He frequently writes articles on Java and related technologies. Tarun has also authored multiple online courses, including a best-selling course on the YAML data serialization language.

He has presented technical lectures at several developer conferences, including SAP TechEd and the Great Indian Developer Summit. He has been presenting at conferences for more than 15 years and actively publishes technical papers and blogs to assist everyone in grasping the fundamentals of software technology. Tarun developed cloud-based video conferencing applications using a microservices architecture with the Spring framework and has experience working with Persistence APIs and the Hazelcast framework for building REST-based services.

He also developed many end-to-end cloud-based solutions using various architectural patterns, including microservices and service-oriented architectures. Tarun has gained expertise in web, mobile, and cloud technologies. He is also knowledgeable in applied agile methodologies, including user-centric and mobile-first design for managing projects with cross-functional teams located in multiple geographies. Tarun is the co-author of *Java EE to Jakarta EE 10 Recipes: A Problem-Solution Approach for Enterprise Java* (Apress, 2022).

Having previously worked in Canada and Germany, Tarun currently resides in Hyderabad, India with his wife and son. You can follow him on LinkedIn (`www.linkedin.com/in/taruntelang/`), Facebook (`www.facebook.com/tarun.telang`), and Twitter (@taruntelang). His blog at `https://blogs.taruntelang.me` is an excellent resource for all things related to software technology!

About the Technical Reviewers

 **Massimo Nardone** has more than 25 years of experience in security, web/mobile development, cloud, and IT architecture. His true IT passions are security and Android. He has been programming and teaching others how to program with Android, Perl, PHP, Java, VB, Python, C/C++, and MySQL for more than 20 years. He holds a Master of Science degree in computing science from the University of Salerno, Italy.

He has worked as a CISO, CSO, security executive, IoT executive, project manager, software engineer, research engineer, chief security architect, PCI/SCADA auditor, and senior lead IT security/cloud/SCADA architect for many years. His technical skills include security, Android, cloud, Java, MySQL, Drupal, Cobol, Perl, web and mobile development, MongoDB, D3, Joomla, Couchbase, C/C++, WebGL, Python, Pro Rails, Django CMS, Jekyll, Scratch, and more.

He was a visiting lecturer and supervisor for exercises at the Networking Laboratory of the Helsinki University of Technology (Aalto University). He also holds four international patents (in the PKI, SIP, SAML, and Proxy areas). He is currently working for Cognizant as head of cybersecurity and CISO to help clients in areas of information and cybersecurity, including strategy, planning, processes, policies, procedures, governance, awareness, and so forth. In June, 2017, he became a permanent member of the ISACA Finland Board.

Massimo has reviewed more than 45 IT books for different publishing companies and is the co-author of *Pro Spring Security: Securing Spring Framework 5 and Boot 2-based Java Applications* (Apress, 2019), *Beginning EJB in Java EE 8* (Apress, 2018), *Pro JPA 2 in Java EE 8* (Apress, 2018), and *Pro Android Games* (Apress, 2015)

Pramit Das has more than 12 years of experience in software design and development across multiple platforms using various technology stacks. He is extremely passionate about programming and exploring new and upcoming technologies. He has extensive hands-on experience with programming languages like C/C++, Java, Scala, JavaScript, and Python, along with their respective tools, libraries, and frameworks, including Spring, Django, NodeJs, and Spark. He also has excellent knowledge of backend storage solutions from Oracle, MySQL, MongoDB, and Cassandra, as well as other cloud-based managed services.

Academically, Pramit received his Bachelor's of Technology from NIT, Rourkela in Computer Science & Engineering, graduating in 2009. He has experience in product- and service-based industries and is currently working for the cloud giant Salesforce as a full-time engineer.

Acknowledgments

I would like to thank my wife, Nikita, and son, Vihan, for their patience and love throughout the process of writing this book. I am indebted to all my mentors and friends who encouraged me to keep on growing during every phase of my professional career.

I'd like to thank my parents for pushing me in the right direction with technology and always supporting me every step of the way, even when I decided to do something completely different than they expected. It's also important to note that without them, I probably wouldn't have become a developer and had such a great career. Lastly, thanks again go out to my wife (and soulmate), Nikita. It's an incredible feeling to be with someone who keeps you motivated and challenges you, not only professionally but personally.

Thank you for always being there for me!

I'd like to send a special thanks to Pramit Das and Massimo Nardone (technical reviewers), for their impeccable work on this book. I also greatly appreciate Steve Anglin, Mark Powers, and everyone at Apress Media (apress.com) for their support in getting this book published.

Last, but not least, I would like to thank you, the reader, for taking the time to read this book. I hope that it will help you in your journey of becoming a better Jakarta EE developer.

Introduction

Cloud-native applications are becoming increasingly popular due to their many benefits, such as scalability, flexibility, and efficiency. Cloud-native applications are designed to take advantage of the cloud paradigm. It means that they are distributed, scalable, resilient, and elastic. You can run them on public, private, or hybrid clouds. To build cloud-native applications, developers must use the right tools and technologies.

Enterprise Java (or Jakarta Enterprise Edition) is a popular platform for cloud-native applications. It provides a set of standards and APIs that help developers build enterprise-grade applications. Many platform vendors, including Red Hat, IBM, and Oracle, support this standard. It offers a number features that make it an ideal choice for developing cloud-native applications.

The MicroProfile initiative was started in 2016 by Red Hat, IBM, Tomitribe, and Payara. The group aims to improve the application developer experience in a microservices environment by providing a baseline platform definition that multiple runtimes can implement. The group released the first version of the MicroProfile specification in June, 2016. The specification includes a set of APIs for application developers, including RESTful web services, context and dependency injection, and JSON processing.

MicroProfile is a set of specifications that define how developers can use Jakarta EE to build microservices. It also provides a platform that helps developers create cloud-native applications. MicroProfile is aligning its specifications with the Jakarta EE platform. The goal of the MicroProfile group is to create a set of standards that developers can use to develop microservices on top of the Jakarta EE platform. The Eclipse Foundation, the home of the Jakarta EE project, also manages the creation of MicroProfile standards.

MicroProfile is a Jakarta EE Working Group. It was created in response to the popularity of microservices. It also addresses the need for a standard platform for developing microservices. It initially consisted of a few Jakarta EE vendors (IBM, Red Hat, Payara, and Tomitribe) and has grown to include more than 25 members, including Oracle, Microsoft, Hazelcast, and more. The Eclipse Foundation governs the MicroProfile initiative, and the MicroProfile specification is developed through the Eclipse

MicroProfile project. The project is open to all individuals and organizations that want to contribute. The MicroProfile specification is developed openly and transparently, and all contributions are welcomed. The Eclipse MicroProfile project uses a collaborative development process, and all interested parties are encouraged to participate.

Docker is a software container platform that allows developers to package an application with all its dependencies into a standardized unit for software development. You can run Docker containers on any platform, including public, private, and hybrid clouds. It makes it easy to deploy applications on any platform, including cloud platforms. Docker is a popular open-source container platform that you can use to package and run microservices. It provides several advantages over traditional virtualization technologies, including portability, ease of use, and more.

Kubernetes is a tool for managing containerized applications. It provides an open-source platform for deploying, managing, and scaling applications. Kubernetes is based on the Linux kernel and can use Docker containers to manage applications. It provides features such as scaling, load balancing, and self-healing.

Kubernetes automates the deployment, scaling, and management of containerized apps. It supports easy management and discovery of your applications by grouping containers into logical units. Kubernetes is built on decades of experience at Google running production workloads at scale, as well as adopting the best-of-breed ideas and practices from the community.

Kubernetes is portable and extensible, allowing it to run anywhere, from your laptop to public clouds to data centers. The simplicity and flexibility of Kubernetes make it an excellent choice for cloud-native applications. In addition, it's open-source software, allowing you to take advantage of community innovations.

Kubernetes is production-ready, with robust features and capabilities to orchestrate your containerized applications. Kubernetes has been battle-tested at scale, running some of the largest sites in the world.

In this book, you learn how to use MicroProfile and Jakarta EE technologies to develop microservices, deploy them on Kubernetes/Docker, and create cloud-native applications. The book also covers best practices for developing cloud-native applications with MicroProfile and Jakarta EE. It starts by looking at the different aspects of cloud-native applications. You will then move on to setting up your development environment and learning about the basics of Jakarta EE. Next, the book explores the features of MicroProfile and you'll learn how to use them to build microservices.

You will then learn about Docker and Kubernetes and how to use them to deploy your applications. Finally, you will put everything together and learn how to build a complete cloud-native application.

Who This Book Is For

Welcome to *Beginning Cloud Native Development with MicroProfile, Jakarta EE, and Kubernetes.*

This book is for Java developers who want to learn how to develop cloud-native applications using MicroProfile and Jakarta EE. No prior knowledge of Kubernetes or container orchestration is required.

In this book, you learn how to develop cloud-native applications using MicroProfile and Jakarta EE and deploy them to Kubernetes. The book covers topics such as writing RESTful web services, creating microservices, configuring health checks, and more.

By the end of this book, you will be able to develop cloud-native applications using MicroProfile and Jakarta EE and deploy them to Kubernetes.

How This Book Is Structured

This book covers four main topics.

- **Cloud-native development** introduces the concept of cloud-native development and the twelve-factor app methodology. You learn about the benefits of developing cloud-native applications and the challenges you must consider when migrating existing applications to the cloud.

- **MicroProfile specifications** provides an overview of the MicroProfile specifications and how they can be used to develop microservices. You learn about the different types of annotations available and how to use them to create RESTful web services.

- **Jakarta EE specifications** introduces the Jakarta EE platform and its various specifications. You learn about the differences between Java EE and Jakarta EE and the new features available on the platform.

- **Kubernetes** covers the basics of container orchestration with Kubernetes. You learn about the different types of objects created in a Kubernetes cluster, how to deploy applications to Kubernetes, and how to scale applications using Kubernetes.

Conventions

Throughout the book, I use a consistent style for presenting Java code, SQL, command-line text, and results. When pieces of code, SQL, reserved words, or code fragments are presented in the text, they are presented in fixed-width Courier font, such as this (working) example:

```
public class MyExample {
    public static void main(String[] args){
        System.out.println("Jakarta EE is excellent!");
    }
}
```

Downloading the Code

The code examples in this book are available at github.com/apress/beginning-cloud-native-dev-microprofile-jakarta-kubernetes.

Note The sources for this book may change over time, in order to incorporate the most up-to-date features in Jakarta EE, MicroProfile, and the Kubernetes platform. If you find any issues in the sources, please submit them via the book's GitHub repo and the code will be adjusted accordingly.

CHAPTER 1

Introduction to Cloud Computing

Cloud computing is the latest buzzword in the technology industry, and for good reason. It has the potential to revolutionize the way people use computers. This chapter introduces cloud computing and explains what it is. You will also look at some examples of cloud computing and learn about the benefits of using this new technology. Finally, you will explore the different types of cloud computing and see how they have evolved over time.

Introduction to Cloud Computing

Cloud computing is a type of computing where resources, such as applications and data, are stored on remote servers and accessed over the Internet. Instead of having a program installed on your computer, you can access or keep programs on a remote server. As a result, you can access your data from any device with an Internet connection, whether it's a desktop computer, laptop, tablet, or smartphone.

Cloud computing has the following key benefits. It enables ubiquitous, convenient, on-demand network access to a shared pool of configurable computing resources (e.g., networks, servers, storage, applications, and services) that can be rapidly provisioned and released with minimal management effort or service provider interaction. Figure 1-1 illustrates how end-users access cloud computing.

© Tarun Telang 2023

T. Telang, *Beginning Cloud Native Development with MicroProfile, Jakarta EE, and Kubernetes*, https://doi.org/10.1007/978-1-4842-8832-0_1

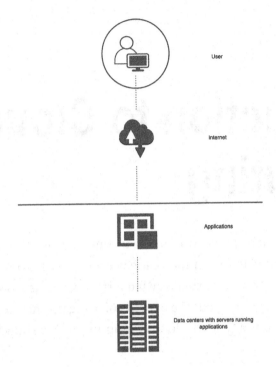

User

Internet

Applications

Data centers with servers running applications

Figure 1-1. *Cloud computing*

Cloud computing also has environmental benefits because it reduces the need for energy-intensive hardware.

Examples of Cloud Computing

There are many different examples of cloud computing, but some of the most common ones include:

- **Email:** *Gmail, Yahoo Mail,* and *Outlook.com* are all examples of email services that are based in the cloud. This means that you can check your email on your smartphone, tablet, or desktop computer, regardless of where you are in the world. The ability to access your email from any device with an Internet connection is an example of cloud computing. This is an excellent feature if you need to check your email while you're on vacation or traveling for work. Further, if you accidentally delete an email, it can be quickly recovered from the cloud.

- **Cloud storage:** *Dropbox, Google Drive,* and *iCloud* are all examples of cloud storage services. This means that instead of storing files on your computer, you can store them online. This gives you the ability to access those files from any device with an Internet connection.

- **Web-based productivity software:** *Google Docs, Sheets,* and *Slides* are all examples of productivity software that is based in the cloud. This means that instead of having a program installed on your computer, you can create and edit documents, spreadsheets, and presentations from any device with an Internet connection. Cloud storage is better than having documents on your computer because you can access them from any device that has an Internet connection. This is helpful if you need to work on a document from different places or if you accidentally delete one. Additionally, cloud storage makes it easier for people to collaborate on projects because they can all work on the document simultaneously without having to worry about emailing each other versions of the document.

- **Multimedia streaming:** Netflix, Vimeo, and YouTube are all examples of video streaming services, whereas Spotify, Apple Music, and Pandora are all examples of music streaming services that are based in the cloud. This means that instead of downloading media (video or song) to your computer, you can watch it from any device with an Internet connection. Media streaming is popular because it doesn't take up any space on your device, and you can watch videos without waiting for them to download. Figure 1-2 shows different types of cloud computing applications. These are just a few examples of cloud computing. As you can see, cloud computing can be very helpful in various ways.

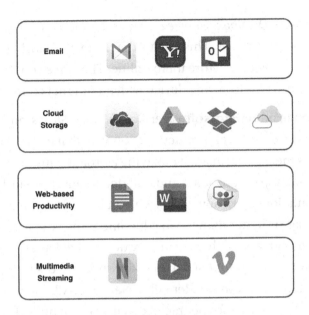

Figure 1-2. Cloud computing application types

Benefits of Cloud Computing

In recent years, the use of cloud computing has grown exponentially. This is because cloud computing can provide several benefits, such as the following:

- **Cost savings:** Cloud computing can save you money on hardware and software costs. For example, you can use a cloud-based storage service instead of buying a physical hard drive. Cloud-based storage can be more cost-effective than buying a physical hard drive. This is because you don't have to buy expensive hardware, like a computer. You also save money on software costs by using a cloud-based application instead of buying a software program for your local machine. This is a significant benefit of cloud-based solutions—you don't have to worry about capital expenditure for hardware and software, regular patching, or data center upkeep. The provider takes care of all of these tasks. This can save you time and money, and it makes it easy to get started with cloud computing.

- **Flexibility and scalability:** Cloud computing gives you the ability to scale your resources up or down, depending on your needs. For

4

example, if you have a sudden increase in traffic to your website, you can quickly add more servers to handle the load. On the other hand, if you have decreased traffic, you can remove servers to save on costs. This can also save you money on your computing costs.

- **Reliability:** Cloud-based services are more reliable than on-premises solutions. This is because cloud providers have the resources and expertise to ensure that their services are always up and running. Cloud services are distributed across multiple servers, so there is no single point of failure. The data is replicated across multiple servers across multiple availability zones, so if one server goes down, the others can pick up the slack. They have a disaster recovery plan in place, which helps ensure that your data is always safe and accessible.

- **Productivity:** Cloud computing can improve your team's productivity by giving it the ability to access information and applications from anywhere in the world.

Essential Characteristics of Cloud Computing

The cloud computing model comprises five essential characteristics, as shown in Figure 1-3. They are on-demand self-service, broad network access, resource pooling, rapid elasticity, and measured service. Let's look at each of these characteristics in detail.

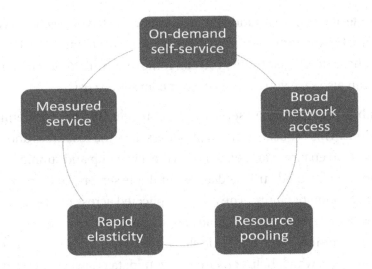

Figure 1-3. *Essential characteristics of cloud computing*

On-Demand Self-Service

Users can access the cloud services without interacting with the service provider. They can simply sign up for a service through a web-based interface and start using it immediately. For example, users can sign up for cloud services and start using them to store their data without needing to contact customer support. This characteristic enables users to get started with cloud services quickly and easily without needing complex configuration.

Broad Network Access

Cloud services can be accessed over a network using any standard devices, such as laptops, smartphones, and tablets. For example, users can access their cloud storage accounts from anywhere in the world using their laptops or smartphones. This characteristic makes cloud services very convenient and accessible.

Resource Pooling

The cloud provider pools the resources like storage, processing, memory, and network bandwidth from multiple customers and makes them available on demand. Multi-tenancy is a crucial feature of cloud computing that enables providers to share resources among multiple customers. In this model, each customer is given a dedicated portion of the resources and is isolated from other customers. This helps providers manage and monitor the resources more effectively and provides customers with added security and privacy. This characteristic also enables efficient utilization of resources and reduces the cost of ownership.

Rapid Elasticity

Cloud services can be quickly scaled up or down to meet the changing needs of the users. In some cases, consumers may automatically be able to scale their usage up or down, depending on the cloud provider's policies. For example, a social networking site may need to quickly add more servers during a significant event, such as an election or a natural disaster. In other cases, users may need to scale down their usage to save costs. This characteristic enables cloud providers to allocate resources dynamically with the flexibility to increase or decrease their usage as required.

Measured Service

Cloud providers offer metered services that are charged according to their actual usage. In addition, cloud systems can automatically control and optimize resources by leveraging a pattern in metering. For example, a cloud storage service may automatically move data to cheaper storage tiers when it is not accessed for a specific period. This characteristic provides users with greater control over their usage and costs.

Types of Cloud Computing Based on Deployment Models

There are four main types of cloud computing: public, community, private, and hybrid. Figure 1-4 shows each of these different types of cloud computing based on deployment models.

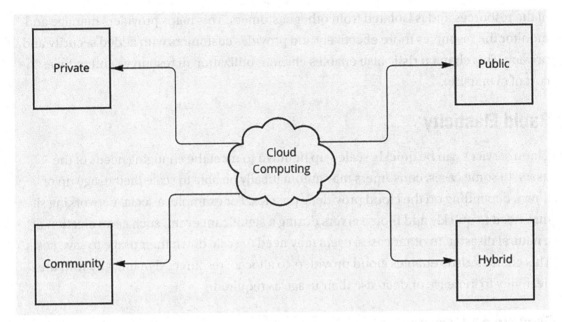

Figure 1-4. Types of cloud computing based on deployment models

The following sections discuss each type of cloud computing in detail.

Public Cloud

A public cloud is a type of cloud computing that delivers hosted services over the Internet. Public clouds are owned and operated by third-party companies that provide their resources—such as servers, storage, and applications—to customers on demand. The most common examples of public clouds are Gmail and Dropbox. These services allow users to access their data and applications from any device with an Internet connection.

Benefits of a Public Cloud

The main advantage of using a public cloud is that it's highly scalable, and you only pay for the resources you use. For example, you can buy more storage space if you need to store more data in Gmail. Public clouds are also convenient because they can be accessed from anywhere worldwide.

Drawbacks of a Public Cloud

The main disadvantage of using a public cloud is that you're relying on the cloud provider's security measures. For example, if Dropbox were to experience a data breach, your data would be at risk. Additionally, public clouds can be less reliable than private clouds because they are subject to outages beyond the cloud provider's control.

Community Cloud

A community cloud is a computing model that delivers shared applications and data to a community of users with common requirements or objectives. It promotes collaboration, flexibility, and standardization within the community while providing users access to a personalized, self-service environment. The cloud infrastructure is provisioned for exclusive use by a specific community of consumers from organizations with shared concerns (e.g., mission, security requirements, policy, and compliance considerations).

The community cloud model can be used to support a variety of communities, including those that are:

- **Technical**: Developers, engineers, or other technically-focused users who share joint development or operational objectives.

- **Business-based**: Employees in the same company or organization who need to collaborate on projects or access shared data.

- **Geographic**: People who live in the same region or city and want to connect online.

- **Interest-based**: Users with a common interest or hobby who want to connect and share information.

Community clouds are often established by organizations or users who come together to pool resources and create a shared infrastructure. This infrastructure can be used to host applications, store data, or provide other services to members of the community. In many cases, community clouds are managed by a third-party provider who is responsible for maintaining the underlying infrastructure.

Benefits of a Community Cloud

A community cloud can offer many benefits to users, including:

- **Reduced costs:** By sharing resources and pooling expenses, users can save money on computing costs.

- **Improved collaboration:** A community cloud can make it easier for users to collaborate on projects or access shared data.

- **Enhanced security:** A community cloud can provide users with improved security and privacy protection.

- **improved performance:** By sharing resources, a community cloud can improve the performance of applications and services for users.

Generally, a community cloud shares infrastructure between several organizations from a specific group or sector with similar concerns (security, compliance, jurisdiction, etc.), who have decided to cooperate to optimize their resource utilization and reduce costs. Typically, each organization uses its portion of the community cloud infrastructure and pays according to its actual use.

Limitations of a Community Cloud

A community cloud can be a powerful tool for organizations that need to share data or collaborate on projects. Still, it is essential to consider the potential risks and benefits before implementing this solution. In some cases, a community cloud may not be the best option for an organization, mainly if there are concerns about security or privacy.

Organizations should also consider the following factors when deciding whether to implement a community cloud:

- Does my organization have the necessary resources to manage a community cloud?

- Are there any security or privacy concerns that need to be considered?

- What are the costs associated with implementing a community cloud?

- What are the benefits of using a community cloud?

- Are there any potential risks associated with using a community cloud?

A community cloud can be a great way to improve collaboration and reduce costs, but it's essential to consider the potential risks and benefits before implementing this solution.

Private Cloud

The private cloud is a type of cloud computing that delivers similar advantages to the public cloud, including scalability and self-service, but through a proprietary architecture.

A private cloud is built on a private network and offers more security and control than a public cloud. When an organization opts for private cloud deployment, it can keep its data and applications in-house or outsource it to a third-party provider.

Private clouds are owned and operated by a single organization. This means that only members of that organization can access the service.

Benefits of a Private Cloud

There are several benefits of using a private cloud, including:

- **Increased security and control:** Private clouds offer increased security and control over public clouds deployed on a private network.

- **Improved performance:** Private clouds can offer improved performance, as they are not shared with other organizations.

- **Reduced costs:** Private clouds can be more cost-effective than public clouds, especially for organizations with the necessary infrastructure.

Disadvantages of a Private Cloud

Despite these benefits, there are also some challenges associated with private clouds.

- Private clouds can be more complex to deploy and manage than public clouds. Additionally, private clouds may require a larger upfront investment.

- Organizations should carefully consider their needs before deciding whether a private cloud is the correct solution.

Private clouds are not suitable for everyone, but they can be an excellent option for organizations that require increased security and control or improved performance. Private clouds are often used by large organizations, such as banks and government agencies.

Hybrid Cloud

A hybrid cloud combines an on-premises infrastructure—or a private cloud—with a public cloud. This combination can help organizations access data and applications more easily and securely while maintaining control over sensitive data. Hybrid clouds are often used by organizations that need to keep specific data confidential. One example of a hybrid cloud is an organization that stores some data and applications on a private cloud and other data on a public cloud. This combination can help organizations access data and applications more easily and securely while maintaining stricter control over sensitive data.

Benefits of a Hybrid Cloud

There are several benefits to using a hybrid cloud, including:

- **Increased flexibility:** Organizations can more easily scale their resources up or down as needed with a hybrid cloud. This can be helpful during times of increased demand, such as during a product launch or holiday shopping season.

- **Improved security:** By keeping sensitive data on a private cloud, organizations can better protect it from potential threats.

- **Reduced costs:** Organizations can save money by using a hybrid cloud, as they can take advantage of the lower costs associated with public clouds while still maintaining control over their data.

Drawbacks of a Hybrid Cloud

There are also some potential drawbacks to using a hybrid cloud, including:

- **Complicated management:** Managing a private and public cloud can be complex. Organizations need staff with the knowledge and expertise to manage both types of environments.

- **Increased costs:** While hybrid clouds can save organizations money, they can also cost more than a private or public cloud alone. This is because organizations need to maintain and manage two separate environments.

- **Potential security risks:** Although hybrid clouds can offer improved security, there is still the potential for data breaches. This is because data is stored in both public and private environment, increasing the chances that unauthorized individuals could access it.

A hybrid cloud provides many benefits for organizations, including increased flexibility, improved security, and reduced costs. However, there are also potential drawbacks, such as complicated management and increased costs. Overall, a hybrid cloud is a good option for organizations that need to maintain control over their data while taking advantage of the lower costs associated with public clouds.

Service Models of Cloud Computing

As you have now learned about the essential characteristics of cloud computing, this section covers the service models of cloud computing. These service models are different modes in which cloud services can be delivered. Figure 1-5 shows the three most common types of cloud services, which are Infrastructure as a Service (IaaS), Platform as a Service (PaaS), and Software as a Service (SaaS).

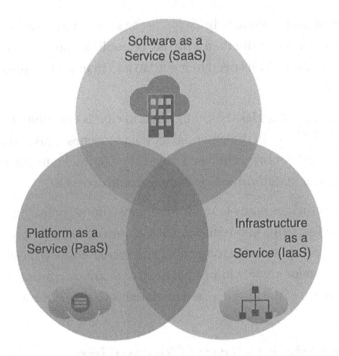

Figure 1-5. *Service models of cloud computing*

The following sections look at each of these service models in detail.

Software as a Service (SaaS)

Software as a Service (SaaS) is a type of cloud computing that delivers software applications over the Internet. SaaS is a way for businesses to save money on IT infrastructure and reduce the complexity of managing software applications.

With SaaS, businesses can access and use software applications hosted in the cloud. This means that businesses don't have to install or manage the infrastructure required to run the software. SaaS applications are typically accessed via a web browser or a mobile app.

The capability provided to the consumer is to use the provider's applications running on a cloud infrastructure. The applications are accessible from various client devices through either a thin client interface, such as a web browser (e.g., web-based email), or a program interface. The consumer does not manage or control the underlying cloud infrastructure, including network, servers, operating systems, storage, or even individual application capabilities, with the possible exception of limited user-specific application configuration settings.

Benefits

There are many benefits of using SaaS, including:

- **Reduced costs:** With SaaS, businesses only pay for the software they use on a subscription basis. There is no need to invest in hardware or IT infrastructure.

- **Increased flexibility:** SaaS applications can be accessed from any device with an Internet connection. This makes it easy for businesses to scale their usage up or down as needed.

- **Improved security:** SaaS providers typically have strong security measures in place to protect data.

Disadvantages

While SaaS can offer many benefits, there are also some issues to be aware of, including:

- **Vendor lock-in:** Once a business uses a SaaS application, it can be challenging to switch to another provider. This is because data is often stored in the cloud, and switching providers can be complex and expensive.

- **Limited customization:** SaaS applications are typically not as customizable as on-premises software. This can make it challenging to meet the specific needs of a business.

- **Internet dependency:** SaaS applications require an Internet connection to work. This can be an issue for businesses with poor Internet connectivity.

Despite these issues, SaaS is a popular option for businesses of all sizes. It can be a cost-effective and flexible way to improve business operations.

How It Works

To understand how SaaS works, it is helpful to know a little about the architecture of SaaS applications. SaaS applications are typically built using a multi-tier architecture. This means that the application is divided into multiple parts:

- **The frontend:** This is the part of the application that users interact with.

- **The backend:** This is the part of the application that stores data and handles the logic.

- **The middleware:** This is the part of the application that connects the frontend and backend. It is typically built using a web application framework.

SaaS applications are hosted in the cloud, which means that they are stored on a network of servers. When users want to use the application, they send a request to the server. The server then sends the frontend code to the user's device. The user's device then runs the code and displays the frontend of the application. When users interact with the application, their interactions are sent to the backend. The backend then processes the request and sends a response back to the user's device.

Platform as a Service (PaaS)

PaaS is a cloud computing service that provides users with a platform for developing, testing, and deploying applications in the cloud. PaaS services can be delivered in various ways, including through a web-based interface, an API, or a command-line interface.

PaaS is an excellent solution for developers who want to focus on building applications without having to worry about managing infrastructure. PaaS providers take care of all the underlying infrastructure so that developers can concentrate on their code. In addition, PaaS services are often scalable and provide high availability, making them ideal for mission-critical applications.

The developers don't manage or control the underlying cloud infrastructure, including networks, servers, operating systems, or storage, but have control over the deployed applications and possibly over the application hosting environment configurations.

Benefits of PaaS

Consider these advantages offered by PaaS:

- **Reduced time to market for new applications:** Since PaaS takes care of all the underlying infrastructure, developers can focus on building their applications, leading to a faster market lead time.

- **Cost savings:** PaaS services are often more cost-effective than traditional application development and deployment models since you only pay for what you use.

- **Increased developer productivity:** PaaS services can increase developer productivity by providing them with everything they need to develop and deploy applications in the cloud.

- **Improved application quality:** PaaS services can help improve the quality of your applications by providing access to the latest tools and technologies.

- **Increased agility and flexibility:** PaaS services can provide you with the agility and flexibility you need to respond to changing market conditions quickly.

PaaS services have recently become a popular solution for organizations of all sizes who want to take advantage of the benefits of cloud computing. Whether you're looking to reduce costs, increase developer productivity, or improve application quality, PaaS can help you achieve your goals.

Limitations of PaaS

When choosing a PaaS provider, it's important to consider your specific needs and requirements. Make sure to carefully read the provider's terms of service to ensure that your use case is supported. In addition, be aware of the following potential limitations of PaaS:

- **Vendor lock-in:** Once you've developed your application on a specific PaaS platform, it can be difficult and costly to migrate to another platform. If your PaaS provider goes out of business or raises prices significantly, this can be a problem.

- **Lack of control:** Since you don't have control over the underlying infrastructure, you may be limited in how you can customize and configure your applications.

- **Security risks associated with shared infrastructure:** Since PaaS services share infrastructure with other customers, there is a risk that your data could be compromised.

- **Limited choice of tools and technologies:** Some PaaS providers only offer a limited selection of tools and technologies, which may not be suitable for your needs.

Infrastructure as a Service (IaaS)

IaaS refers to the provision of computing infrastructure—typically physical or virtual machines—and associated services usually delivered over the Internet. IaaS providers offer customers a pay-as-you-go model for using, managing, and scaling these resources.

IaaS provides customers with on-demand access to a pool of computing, storage, and networking resources. These resources can be rapidly provisioned and released with minimal management effort or service provider interaction.

IaaS enables businesses to quickly scale their computing infrastructure up or down, as needed. This flexibility is one of the key benefits of IaaS.

IaaS providers offer a variety of services, including:

- Compute (virtual and bare-metal servers)

- Storage (object, block, and file storage)

- Networking (load balancing, VPN, and DNS)

- Monitoring and management (logging, performance monitoring, and security monitoring)

- Security (firewalls, intrusion detection/prevention, and compliance)

Benefits of IaaS

Some of the other benefits of IaaS include:

- **Reduced capital expenditure:** Customers only pay for the resources they use, when they use them. There is no need to make a large upfront investment in hardware and software.

- **Flexibility and scalability:** Resources can be quickly scaled up or down to meet changing needs.

- **Reduced operational expenditure:** IaaS customers don't have to worry about managing and maintaining their infrastructure. This is the responsibility of the service provider.

- **Pay per use:** Customers only pay for the resources they use when they use them.

Limitations of IaaS

IaaS is not without its limitations. These include:

- **Limited control:** Customers do not have direct control over the physical infrastructure.

- **Security concerns:** Customers are responsible for the security of their data and applications.

- **Vendor lock-in:** Customers may be locked into a particular vendor's platform, making it difficult to switch to a different vendor in the future.

The Role of Java in Cloud Computing

Java plays a very important role in cloud computing. There are several reasons why Java is a good choice for developing cloud-based applications.

1. **Java is a very stable language:** It has been around for over 25 years and is used by some of the biggest companies in the world, such as Google, Amazon, and IBM. This means that there is a large community of developers who are familiar with the language and can provide support.

2. **Java is very scalable:** Java can be used to create programs for large businesses. Many people know how to use it and can help you if you have any problems. This means that it can handle large amounts of data and traffic. Cloud-based applications often need to be able to scale quickly and easily, and Java is built for this.

3. **Java is secure:** Security is very important for cloud-based applications. Java has several security features built into the language, which makes it more difficult for hackers to exploit. For example, it has a robust security model that can be used to control access to data and resources.

4. **Java is efficient:** Cloud-based applications need to be able to run quickly and efficiently, and Java is designed for this. The Java Virtual Machine (JVM) is very efficient, and Java code is compiled into bytecode, which is also very efficient.

5. **Java is well supported:** There are many tools and libraries available for Java developers, which makes it easier to develop cloud-based applications.

Note   Java is one of the most popular programming languages in the world, and it has become a key part of cloud computing. Java's popularity is due in part to its platform independence. Java can run on any device or operating system, which makes it a perfect choice for cloud-based applications.

Some of the tools and libraries that can be used to build cloud applications with Java include:

- **Jakarta EE** is a standards-based platform for developing cloud-friendly applications. It provides a comprehensive set of APIs and features that make it easy to develop cloud-based applications.

- **Microprofile** is a lightweight specification that provides a set of APIs and features for developing microservices. It includes features such as health checking, configuration, and security.

As per the TIOBE Index (`https://www.tiobe.com/tiobe-index/`), Java is currently the third most popular language after Python and C. It has been in the top three since 2002 and shows no signs of falling anytime soon. This is due to its large and loyal user base, as well as the many features that make it ideal for developing cloud-based applications.

It is also the most popular language for developing cloud-based applications, according to a survey of global enterprise developers and decision-makers by Cloud Foundry (`www.cloudfoundry.org/wp-content/uploads/Developer-Language-Report_FINAL.pdf`). In conclusion, Java is a good choice for developing cloud-based applications because it is stable, scalable, secure, efficient, and well-supported.

The Evolution of Cloud Computing

Cloud computing can be traced back to the early days of the Internet when researchers at universities and companies were looking for ways to share resources. This included sharing computer time, storage, and applications. They used the term "utility computing" to describe this concept. In early 1989, a project called the World Wide Web was developed by Tim Burners-Lee, which allowed users to access information over the Internet. This led to the development of web-based applications hosted on central servers.

HTML and HTTP were developed to provide a standard way to share documents and data. HTML is a markup language that is used to create web pages. It provides a way to structure information and includes tags that can control a web page's appearance. HTML is not a programming language, but it can be used to create pages that include JavaScript and other scripting languages.

HTTP is a protocol that transfers data between a web server and a web browser. It is the foundation of the World Wide Web and provides a way for browsers to request information from servers and for servers to send information back to browsers. HTTP is an application layer protocol that operates on top of TCP/IP, the primary communications protocol of the Internet.

In 1994, Netscape released the first commercial web browser, making the Internet more accessible to the public. As a result, the demand for web-based applications increased. Shortly after, in 1995, Sun Microsystems released the first version of Java. Java runs on a virtual machine, allowing it to run on any operating system.

Java's platform independence is one of its key features, making it a perfect choice for developing web-based applications.

In the early 2000s, a new type of service known as a web service began to emerge. Web services are applications that provide a specific functionality over the Internet. In those days web services were simple, such as a weather service that provided the current temperature for a given location. As the popularity of web services increased, so did the demand for more complex web services. In response to this demand, companies began to offer web-based application platforms.

The first generation of application platforms was focused on providing the infrastructure needed to run web services. This included a web server, a database, and an application server. The second generation of application platforms added support for more complex web-based applications. These platforms included features such as security, scalability, and manageability. The second generation of application platforms gave rise to the concept of cloud computing.

For web services to communicate with each other, they need to use a common set of rules. This common set of rules is known as a web service protocol. The two most popular web service protocols are SOAP and REST. SOAP (Simple Object Access Protocol) is a protocol that uses XML to exchange information between applications. REST (Representational State Transfer) is a newer, simpler protocol that uses XML or JSON to exchange information between applications. Most of the web services developed around the early 2000s were created using SOAP. However, in recent years, REST has grown in popularity, as it is simple and easy to use. Figure 1-6 illustrates the evolution of web services.

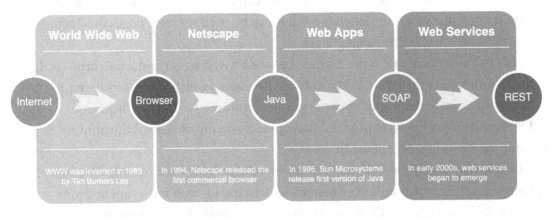

Figure 1-6. Evolution of web services

The first real-world example of cloud computing was launched in the early 2000s by Salesforce.com. They offered a web-based customer relationship management (CRM) application. This allowed businesses to access their CRM data from any device with an Internet connection. In 2008, Google introduced the Google App Engine (GAE), which is a platform that allows developers to build and run applications on the Google Cloud. As a result, cloud computing became more accessible to developers and businesses.

In 2006, Amazon launched Amazon Web Services (AWS), a cloud-based platform allowing developers to build and run applications on the Amazon Cloud. It is a collection of web-based services that allow developers and end-users to access information and applications over the Internet. AWS includes services such as storage, databases, networking, and analytics. As per the ZDNet article (`www.zdnet.com/article/the-top-cloud-providers-of-2021-aws-microsoft-azure-google-cloud-hybrid-saas/`), since its launch, AWS has been the world's largest provider of cloud computing services.

In 2011, Apple launched iCloud, which is a cloud-based storage and synchronization service. It allows users to store data such as documents, music, and photos in the cloud and access them from any Apple device with an Internet connection. Apple iCloud is a closed system, which means that only devices that run iOS or macOS can access it. It is more like a cloud-based storage service similar to Dropbox or Google Drive. In 2008, Microsoft launched Azure, which is a cloud-based platform that allows developers to build and run applications on the Microsoft Cloud. Azure includes services such as storage, databases, networking, and analytics. It is the second most popular cloud computing platform after Amazon Web Services (AWS). Examples of organizations that have migrated to public clouds are Netflix, which uses AWS for its streaming service; and Airbnb, which uses AWS for its vacation rental platform. Azure is more suitable for businesses that use the Microsoft ecosystem of products and services.

The cloud has become the default choice for many organizations. As the use of cloud computing has increased, so have the needs for better tools and technologies to manage and monitor cloud-based applications. In response to this need, a new generation of application platforms has emerged, known as cloud-native applications. Cloud-native applications are designed to be run on the cloud. They are built using microservices, which are small, independent services that can be deployed and scaled independently. Cloud-native applications are also designed to be fault-tolerant and highly available.

In recent years, there has been a shift from traditional Virtual Machines (VMs) to containers for running applications in the cloud. Containers are more lightweight than VMs because they only include the minimum amount of code and libraries needed to run an application. They don't require a lengthy provisioning process like VMs do. This makes it easier to deploy and scale applications in the cloud. They are also more efficient in terms of resources and allow for faster deployment of applications. They are also more portable, as they can run on any platform that supports container runtimes, such as Docker. Docker is the most popular tool for creating and managing containers. It was released in 2013 and has become the standard for running containers in the cloud.

In 2016, the MicroProfile standard was prepared as a collaborative effort by leading software vendors including IBM, Red Hat, Tomitribe, and Payara. It is managed by the Eclipse Foundation. The motivation for creating the MicroProfile specification was to provide a common set of standards for building microservices-based applications that could be run on any Java platform. It includes standards like open tracing, metrics, REST client, JSON processing, JWT-based security, health check monitoring, config, context and dependency injection, RESTful web services, and fault tolerance.

Oracle donated Java EE to the Eclipse Foundation in 2017. The Eclipse Foundation is an open-source community that provides a platform for collaboration and innovation. Jakarta EE specification includes around 40 standards for technologies like servlets, server pages, Jakarta Server Faces, expression language, WebSocket, JSON processing, RESTful web services, security, enterprise beans, batch processing concurrency, transactions, Java Message Service, and many more.

Cloud-native applications are typically deployed on a distributed system and are designed to run on containers. Figure 1-7 illustrates the architecture of a cloud-native application. Containers are more lightweight than virtual machines, but they still require a lot of coordination to run effectively.

Mobile App / Desktop App / Browser

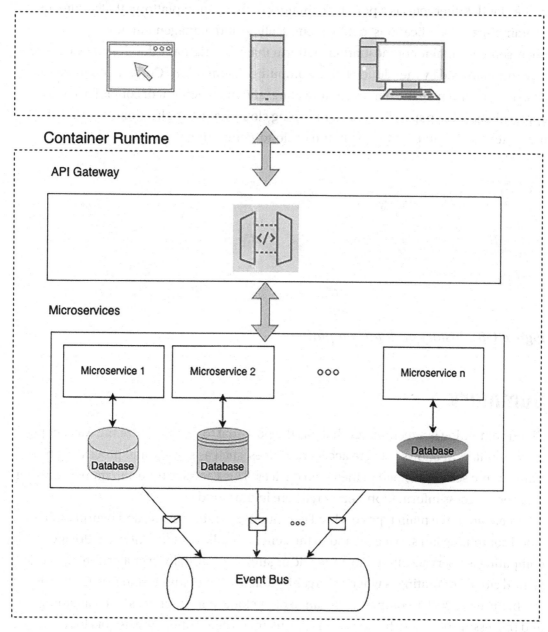

Figure 1-7. *Cloud-native architecture*

Container orchestration is needed because of the complexity of running applications in the cloud. Kubernetes is a popular container orchestration platform that automates container-based applications' deployment, scaling, and management. Kubernetes is an open-source container orchestration platform that was originally developed by Google. It is now managed by the Cloud Native Computing Foundation (CNCF). Kubernetes is designed to automate the deployment, scaling, and management of container-based applications. It is a popular choice for running cloud-native applications. Figure 1-8 illustrates the timeline for the evolution of cloud-computing.

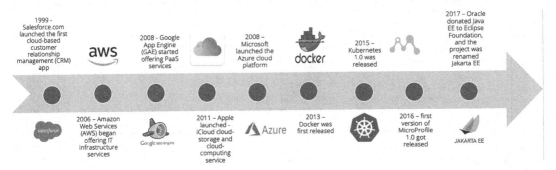

Figure 1-8. *History of cloud computing*

Summary

Cloud computing is a technology that has the potential to revolutionize the way people use computers. It allows users to access resources, such as storage and processing power, from remote servers instead of theit own devices. This can save time and money, making it easier to access information from anywhere in the world.

There are three main types of cloud computing: public, private, and hybrid. Public cloud computing is a service offered to the general public over the Internet. Private cloud computing is a service offered to a specific organization, usually over a private network. Hybrid cloud computing is when an organization uses both public and private clouds.

In the early 2000s, companies began to offer cloud-based services, such as storage and processing power, to businesses and consumers. Since then, the use of cloud computing has grown rapidly, and it is now an essential part of many businesses.

The Java programming language is widely used in cloud computing. It is easy to learn and use and is platform-independent, meaning that programs written in Java can run on any type of computer. Java is also used to create web applications, which are applications that run on a web server and are accessed by users through a web browser.

One of the most important aspects of cloud computing is its use of web services. Web services are applications that can be accessed over the Internet. They are often used to provide a service, such as storage or processing power, to businesses and consumers. Web services are usually written in a programming language such as Java.

Web services use a standard format to communicate data. This makes it possible for different types of computers to understand each other and exchange data. For example, a web service can use Simple Object Access Protocol (SOAP) to communicate with a computer that uses the Windows operating system.

REST (Representational State Transfer) is another type of web service. It is an architectural style for designing networked applications. RESTful web services are based on the principles of REST and use the HTTP protocol to communicate data.

Microservices are a type of software architecture that is designed to make it easy to develop and deploy large applications. Microservices are small, modular components that can be deployed independently. Microservices can be developed in the Java programming language using the various frameworks and standards, like MicroProfiles and Jakarta EE.

You should now have a good understanding of cloud computing. In the next chapter, you learn about cloud-native application development, which allows developers to write code specifically designed to run in the cloud. It uses microservices and containers to make it easy to develop, deploy, and scale applications.

CHAPTER 2

Cloud-Native Application Development

The term "cloud-native" has become ubiquitous in technology circles, but its meaning is still a bit nebulous. To get to the bottom of it, let's start with what it is not: Cloud-native is not about where an application runs. It doesn't matter if an app runs in a public cloud, private cloud, or an on-premises data center. What matters is how the app is built and run. In this chapter, you will start by exploring the meaning of cloud-native, the characteristics of cloud-native applications, the benefits and drawbacks of developing cloud-native apps, and how they differ from traditional apps. Next, you will learn about managed services for Java-based applications and how they play a role in cloud-native app development. Finally, you'll get an overview of the phases of cloud-native app development, including continuous integration/continuous delivery (CI/CD), microservices architecture, containerization, serverless computing, API management, security, and more.

What Is Cloud-Native?

Cloud-native is a term that refers to applications or services that are designed to take advantage of cloud computing environments. Cloud-native applications are typically built using microservices, which are small, independent modules that can be deployed and scaled independently. This approach allows for more flexibility and agility regarding updates and scaling, as each microservice can be updated or scaled individually without affecting the application's other components.

A cloud-native application is designed to take advantage of the elasticity and scalability of the cloud. This approach allows for more flexibility and agility regarding

© Tarun Telang 2023
T. Telang, *Beginning Cloud Native Development with MicroProfile, Jakarta EE, and Kubernetes*, https://doi.org/10.1007/978-1-4842-8832-0_2

updates and scaling, as each microservice can be updated or scaled individually without affecting the other components of the application.

Cloud-native applications are designed to take advantage of the benefits of cloud computing. They are built using a microservices architecture and deployed using containers like Docker and managed Kubernetes clusters. They are also easy to deploy and manage. The term "cloud-native" is often used interchangeably with "container-native" or "microservices-based." Cloud-native applications are a vital part of the cloud computing movement. They allow businesses to rapidly develop and deploy new applications without the need for expensive infrastructure. Cloud-native apps are typically built using open-source technologies such as Docker and Kubernetes.

Java-based cloud-native apps can be built using MicroProfile and Jakarta EE specifications. MicroProfile is an open-source specification that defines a set of standards for building cloud-native applications. It includes standards for microservices, security, and REST APIs.

Jakarta EE is the new name for Java EE, a mature platform for building enterprise applications. MicroProfile and Jakarta EE are complementary. MicroProfile is focused on microservices, while Jakarta EE is focused on enterprise applications. Both platforms can thus be used to build cloud-native applications.

Characteristics of Cloud-Native Applications

If you're looking to build a cloud-native application, there are a few things to keep in mind. First, you need to choose a microservices architecture that will allow you to break your application into small, independent modules. Second, you need to make sure your application is scalable and can handle increased demand by adding more resources. Finally, you need to ensure your application is secure and uses the security features of the cloud platform it is running on.

The following key characteristics are common in cloud-native applications:

- **Microservices:** Cloud-native applications are typically built using microservices, which are small, independent services that work together to form a complete application.

- **Loose coupling:** Cloud-native applications are typically designed with loose coupling, which means that they can be easily divided into smaller parts that can be independently deployed and updated.

- **Scalability:** Cloud-native applications are designed to be scalable, which means they can easily handle increased demand by adding more resources.

- **Resilience:** Cloud-native applications are resilient, which means they can continue functioning even if part of the system fails.

- **Agility:** Cloud-native applications are designed to be agile, which means they can be quickly deployed and updated.

- **Security:** Cloud-native applications are designed to be secure, which means they use the security features of the cloud platform they are running on.

- **Automation:** Cloud-native applications are typically automated, which means that they can be deployed and updated without human intervention.

- **Self-healing:** Cloud-native applications include monitoring and logging features that make detecting and diagnosing problems easy. In addition, cloud-native applications are designed to self-heal, which means they can automatically recover from failures.

- **DevOps culture:** Cloud-native applications are typically developed using a DevOps culture, which means that developers and operations staff work together to create and deploy applications.

These characteristics make cloud-native applications well suited for deployment in cloud environments where resources can be quickly added or removed as needed and where failures are expected. Cloud-native applications can also be quickly updated without affecting the overall system, which makes them ideal for agile development processes.

Figure 2-1 illustrates the key characteristics of cloud-native applications.

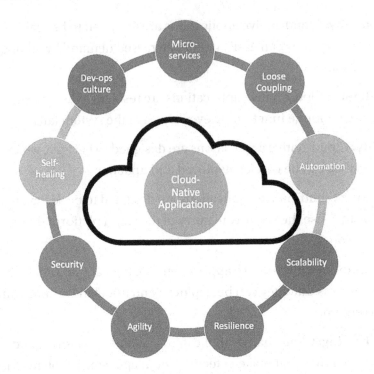

Figure 2-1. *Characteristics of cloud-native applications*

Examples of Cloud-Native Applications

Some popular examples of cloud-native applications include:

- **Netflix:** A cloud-based streaming service that allows users to watch movies and TV shows online.

- **Instagram:** A photo- and video-sharing social networking service that is available on both mobile and web platforms.

- **Pinterest:** A visual discovery and social media tool that allows users to save and share images and videos.

- **Uber:** A ride-sharing service that allows users to request and pay for rides through a mobile app.

- **Airbnb:** A vacation rental marketplace that allows users to find and book vacation rentals.

- **Twitter:** A social networking and microblogging service that allows users to send and receive short updates called "tweets."

- **Facebook:** A social networking service that allows users to connect with friends and family.

- **Spotify:** A music streaming service that gives users access to millions of songs.

These applications are all built using a microservices architecture and deployed using containers. They are designed to be scalable, reliable, and high-performance. For example, Netflix is a cloud-native application built using microservices. Netflix initially used a monolithic architecture, but it transitioned to a microservices-based architecture to take advantage of the scalability and agility of the cloud. Netflix achieved massive scale by breaking its applications into small, independent modules that can be deployed and scaled independently. Netflix also uses containers and a Kubernetes cluster to manage its applications. Containers allow Netflix to package its applications into portable units that can be run anywhere. Kubernetes allows Netflix to deploy and manage its applications at scale quickly.

Benefits of Cloud-Native Applications

Cloud-native development is perfect for businesses that want to rapidly develop and deploy new applications without the need for expensive infrastructure. Cloud-native apps are typically built using open-source technologies such as Docker and Kubernetes. Businesses can enjoy many benefits of using cloud-native applications, including:

- **Scalability:** Cloud-native apps can be quickly scaled up or down to meet changing demands. In other words, they are "elastically" scalable. Cloud-native development is also perfect for businesses that want to take advantage of the scalability and agility of the cloud.

- **Flexibility:** Cloud-native apps can be deployed on a variety of cloud platforms. They are platform-agnostic because they are built using standard technologies such as containers, microservices, and REST APIs. This gives you the flexibility to choose the platform that best meets your needs. Cloud-native apps are built using a microservices architecture, which allows for more flexibility regarding updates and scaling.

- **Reliability:** Cloud-native apps are designed to be highly available and can tolerate failures. This means that they can continue to operate even if there is a failure in one or more of their components. Cloud-native development is also perfect for businesses that want to build high-performance, reliable applications.

- **Performance:** Cloud-native apps are typically high-performance and responsive. This is because they are designed to leverage distributed computing.

- **High availability:** Cloud-native apps are typically available 24/7. They are designed to be deployed on multiple servers.

- **Ease of deployment:** Cloud-native apps can be deployed quickly and easily. They are typically packaged in containers.

In summary, cloud-native applications have all the benefits of cloud computing. Cloud-native applications are designed to take advantage of the elasticity and scalability of the cloud. They are typically built using microservices, which are small, independent modules that can be deployed. Cloud-native apps are scalable, reliable, and high-performance. They are also easy to deploy and manage.

Drawbacks of Using Cloud-Native Applications

There are a few drawbacks of using cloud-native applications to keep in mind. If not done correctly, they can introduce additional complexity and technical debt.

Here are the disadvantages of cloud-native applications:

- **Increased complexity:** They are usually more complex than traditional applications and can be challenging to develop and manage. They often require specialized skills and knowledge to develop and operate effectively.

- **Increased cost:** They can be more expensive to develop and operate than traditional applications due to the need for specialized skills and infrastructure. Additionally, cloud-native applications may require more resources than traditional applications, which can increase costs.

- **Increased dependencies:** They often have more dependencies on other services and components, making them more challenging to manage.

- **More challenging to develop:** They can be more challenging to develop effectively due to the increased complexity. Specialized skills and knowledge are often required.

Despite these drawbacks, cloud-native applications are a good choice for many organizations due to several benefits they offer.

Cloud-Native Applications vs. Traditional Applications

Cloud-native is often contrasted with traditional (legacy) or monolithic applications, which are typically large, complex applications that are difficult to update and scale. Monolithic applications are often not designed to be deployed in cloud environments, which can limit an organization's ability to take advantage of the benefits of the cloud. Table 2-1 lists some of the key differences between a cloud-native application and a traditional application.

Table 2-1. *Key Differences Between Cloud-Native and Traditional Applications*

Characteristics	Cloud-Native Applications	Traditional Applications
Microservices	A cloud-native application is typically built as a set of small, independent microservices.	A traditional application is a single, large codebase deployed as a single unit. In other words, traditional applications use a monolithic architecture.
Loose coupling	Components of a cloud-native application are independently deployable and scalable. They communicate with each other through APIs or messaging queues.	Components of a traditional application are closely dependent on each other. They are difficult to deploy and scale independently.
Automation	Cloud-native applications are built using automation tools, such as continuous integration and continuous delivery (CI/CD) pipelines.	Traditional applications are typically built using manual processes, such as code reviews and testing. They are not built using automation tools, such as continuous integration and continuous delivery (CI/CD) pipelines. This makes them difficult to deploy and scale.
Scalable	Cloud-native applications can be scaled up or down to meet changing demand.	Traditional applications cannot be easily scaled up or down to meet changing demand.
Self-healing	Cloud-native applications are designed to recover from failures automatically.	Traditional applications are not designed to recover from failures automatically.
DevOps culture	Organizations that are using cloud-native applications often have a DevOps culture, which emphasizes collaboration between developers and operations staff to speed up the software development and delivery processes.	This culture shift can be challenging for organizations that are used to more traditional approaches to software development.

Overall, cloud-native applications are designed to be more agile, flexible, and scalable than traditional monolithic applications. They can be a great choice for organizations that are looking to speed up their software development and delivery process.

Cloud-Native Application Development

Cloud-native application development typically follows microservices architecture, in which applications are built as a set of independent, loosely coupled services that can be deployed and scaled independently. Microservices architecture is an approach to software development that favors loose coupling between components. This allows for greater flexibility and agility, as updates to one component do not necessarily require updates to other components. Microservices architecture enables developers to build applications modularly, using small, independent services that can be easily updated and scaled independently. This approach allows for more flexibility and agility when developing and deploying applications. This approach enables developers to make changes to individual services without affecting the entire application.

Organizations are adopting cloud-native application development approaches to accelerate time to market, improve developer productivity, and enable applications to take advantage of the many benefits of the cloud, such as on-demand scalability and reduced operational costs.

Organizations using cloud-native applications have the following advantages:

- They can improve their time to market, as microservices can be deployed independently and quickly.

- They can achieve greater flexibility and scalability, as each microservice can be updated or scaled independently.

- They can reduce operational costs, as they can use elastic compute resources on demand.

In addition to microservices, cloud-native application development relies on several other modern technologies and approaches, including containerization, continuous delivery and deployment, and DevOps.

Organizations that adopt cloud-native application development typically use a combination of public cloud, private cloud, and hybrid cloud environments. This allows them to take advantage of the best of each environment to meet their specific needs.

Cloud-native application development is a rapidly evolving field, and new technologies and approaches are being introduced all the time. As a result, developers need to keep up with the latest advancements to be able to build applications that take full advantage of the cloud.

Cloud-native applications can be built using any programming language. However, some languages are better suited for building cloud-native apps.

Managed Services for Java-Based Applications

Java is a popular choice for building cloud-native applications. This is because it is a mature language with a large ecosystem of tools and libraries. Additionally, many cloud providers offer managed services for Java-based applications. Managed services for Java-based applications are services that help you manage and optimize your Java-based applications. These services can help you with tasks such as monitoring your application's performance, managing your application's dependencies, and managing your application's deployments. Managed services can help you save time and money by automating many of the tasks involved in managing your Java-based applications. Several service providers, including Amazon Web Services, Microsoft Azure, and Google Cloud Platform, also offer services for Java-based applications. Refer to the following resources to learn about the latest offerings in Java from the leading cloud providers:

- Java on Google Cloud (`https://cloud.google.com/java`)

- Java on AWS (`https://aws.amazon.com/java/`)

- Azure for Java developer documentation (`https://docs.microsoft.com/en-us/azure/developer/java/`)

Examples of Cloud-Native Application Development

An example of cloud-native application development is the online retailer Amazon.com. Amazon.com was one of the first companies to adopt a microservices architecture and has been using it for many years. One of the benefits of microservices is that they can be deployed in various environments, including on-premises data centers, public clouds, and hybrid clouds. Amazon has developed its own container service, Amazon Elastic Container Service (ECS), which makes it easy to deploy and manage containers at scale.

As a result, they have been able to build and deploy applications quickly and efficiently and take advantage of the many benefits of the cloud.

Another example of cloud-native application development is the social media platform Twitter. Twitter also adopted a microservices architecture and uses it to deploy new features and updates quickly and efficiently. In addition, Twitter uses continuous delivery and deployment to push out new code changes rapidly and without downtime. Twitter has also developed several techniques for managing and deploying microservices. For example, Twitter used a tool called Murder to manage the deployment of new code changes to its microservices. Murder (referring to a flock of crows) is a distributed system that allows developers to push code changes to a central repository. Then Murder deploys the code changes to the appropriate servers. The Murder tool reduced the time required to deploy new code changes from days to minutes. In addition, Murder also helped reduce the number of outages and bugs that can occur when code changes are deployed manually.

Remember that cloud-native application development is a rapidly evolving field, and new technologies and approaches are being introduced all the time. As a result, you need to keep up with the latest advancements to be able to build applications that take full advantage of the cloud.

Cloud-Native Application Development Is the Future

As the world of technology continues to evolve, so too does the way people develop applications. In recent years, there has been a shift toward cloud-native application development—and for good reason. Cloud-native application development is an approach that takes advantage of the many benefits that the cloud has to offer. By developing applications in this way, you can use the scalability, flexibility and cost-effectiveness that the cloud provides.

In addition, cloud-native application development allows you to take advantage of the latest technologies and trends. By being able to deploy applications in the cloud quickly and easily, you can stay ahead of the curve and continue to meet the ever-changing needs of your users. So, why is cloud-native application development the future of application development? There are many reasons:

- **The cloud provides endless possibilities:** The cloud provides you with an unprecedented level of flexibility and scalability. You can easily deploy applications in the cloud, without having to worry about the infrastructure. This means that you can focus on developing the application, rather than worrying about how to deploy it.

- **The cloud is cost-effective:** The cloud is a cost-effective way to develop and deploy applications. You don't have to worry about maintaining your own infrastructure, which can be costly. In addition, you can take advantage of the pay-as-you-go model, which means that you only pay for the resources that you use.

- **The cloud is always up to date:** The cloud is always up-to-date with the latest technologies and trends. This means that you can take advantage of new features and functionality as soon as they are released.

- **The cloud is global:** The cloud is a global phenomenon. This means that you can reach a global audience with your applications.

- **The cloud is secure:** The cloud is a very secure way to develop and deploy applications. You don't have to worry about the security of your own infrastructure.

So, there you have it—five reasons why cloud-native application development is the future of application development. As the world of technology continues to evolve, the cloud will become increasingly important. If you're not already using the cloud to develop and deploy your applications, now is the time.

Phases of Cloud-Native Application Development

You have learned that there are many benefits to developing cloud-native applications. However, developing cloud-native applications is not without its challenges. One of the biggest challenges is that it requires a complete shift in how developers think about and approach application development. This mindset shift includes viewing applications as services that can be composed of smaller microservices, and being able to deploy these services quickly and easily and in a manner that is consistent with the way the cloud operates. In addition, it is important to be able to manage and monitor these services in order to ensure that they are functioning as intended.

In addition, it can be difficult to find the right tools and technologies to support a cloud-native development process. The good news is that several companies offer cloud-native development platforms and services. These platforms can provide developers with the tools they need to build cloud-native applications. In addition, several open-source projects offer support for cloud-native development. Tools and technologies that support cloud-native app development include container technologies such as Docker, orchestration frameworks such as Kubernetes, and platform as a service (PaaS) offerings that provide pre-built environments for deploying cloud-native applications. There are many open-source PaaS services available that can be used to develop cloud-native applications. Some of these tools include OpenShift, Cloud Foundry, and Heroku.

Table 2-2 shows a list of open-source tools for cloud-native development along with descriptions.

Table 2-2. *Open-Source Tools and PaaS Services for Cloud-Native Application Development*

Tools	Description
Docker	Docker is a tool that enables you to create, deploy, and run applications using containers. Containers allow you to package an application with all of its dependencies so that it can run on any Linux server. This makes it easy to move applications between development, test, and production environments without having to worry about dependencies.
Kubernetes	Kubernetes is an orchestration tool for managing containerized applications. It provides a platform for automating deployment, scaling, and management of containerized applications.
OpenShift	OpenShift is a PaaS offering from Red Hat that provides pre-built environments for deploying cloud-native applications. It includes tools for building, deploying, and managing applications.
Cloud Foundry	Cloud Foundry is an open-source platform as a service (PaaS). It provides a platform for developers to build, deploy, and manage applications. Cloud Foundry is available in a number of different editions, each of which provides a different set of tools and services.
Heroku	Heroku is a PaaS that enables developers to build, deploy, and manage applications. It includes tools for managing application development, deployment, and scaling.

These are just a few of the many tools and technologies that are available for developing cloud-native applications. The most important thing is to choose the right tool for the job at hand. There is no one-size-fits-all solution, so it is important to evaluate the needs of your application and choose the tools that will best support those needs.

Figure 2-2 illustrates the phases of cloud-native application development.

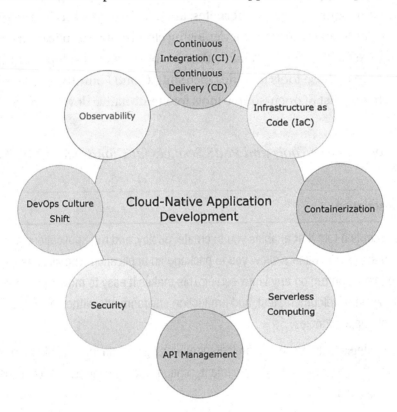

Figure 2-2. *Phases of cloud-native application development*

The next sections covers each phase in detail.

Continuous Integration/Continuous Delivery (CI/CD)

Continuous Integration and Continuous Delivery (CI/CD) is a software engineering practice where members of a team integrate their work frequently, usually each person integrating at least once a day. Each integration is verified by an automated build to detect integration errors as quickly as possible. CD is the practice of shipping code on demand, or more frequently, in order to get feedback from users as soon as possible.

CI/CD automates the development process by integrating code check-ins, automated testing, and software deployment into a single streamlined pipeline. This helps to ensure that code is always checked for errors and conforms to project standards, that tests run automatically to identify potential problems, and that new code is deployed quickly and safely.

CI/CD pipelines are an important part of the modern software development process. They can help speed up the development cycle and make it easier to deploy new code changes.

There are many different CI/CD tools available, but some of the most popular ones include Jenkins, Travis CI (`www.travis-ci.com/`), and CircleCI (`https://circleci.com/`). In addition, there are several cloud-based CI/CD services, such as AWS CodePipeline (`https://aws.amazon.com/codepipeline/`) and Azure DevOps (`https://azure.microsoft.com/en-in/products/devops`).

Infrastructure as Code (IaC)

Infrastructure as Code is an important part of DevOps. It involves managing and automating the deployment of your infrastructure using code. It includes the configuration of servers, networks, and applications. It allows you to define your infrastructure using declarative languages, such as Terraform or AWS CloudFormation. This makes it easy to version-control your infrastructure and automate the provisioning process. In addition, IaC tools can help ensure that your infrastructure is consistent and repeatable, making it easier to manage and update.

IaC can help you manage your infrastructure more effectively, by automating the deployment and management of your resources. This can make it easier to keep your infrastructure consistent and up-to-date, and can help reduce the amount of manual work required to manage your environment.

IaC tools can also help you manage your costs, by allowing you to automate the provisioning and management of your resources. This can help you save money on your infrastructure costs, as well as reduce the time and effort required to manage your environment.

Table 2-3 shows a list of popular IaC tools, along with their descriptions.

Table 2-3. *Popular IaC Tools and Technologies*

IaC Tool/ Technology	Description
AWS CloudFormation	It is a service that helps you model and set up your Amazon Web Services resources so that you can spend less time managing those resources and more time focusing on your applications that run in the cloud. To learn more, visit the AWS Cloud Formation user guide at `https://docs.aws.amazon.com/AWSCloudFormation/latest/UserGuide/Welcome.html`.
Azure Resource Manager	This is a system for managing Azure resources, which makes it easier to deploy and manage your Azure resources. Official document for Azure Resource manager can be found at `https://docs.microsoft.com/en-us/azure/azure-resource-manager/management/overview`.
Google Cloud Deployment Manager	This is a tool that helps you to create, manage, and deploy Google Cloud Platform resources. To learn more about Google Cloud Deployment Manager, visit the official documentation at `https://cloud.google.com/deployment-manager/docs`.
Terraform	This is a tool for building, changing, and versioning infrastructure safely and efficiently. Terraform can manage existing and popular service providers as well as custom in-house solutions. More information about this project can be found at `https://www.terraform.io/`.
Puppet	This is a configuration management tool that helps you automate your infrastructure's provisioning, configuration, and management. Puppet can help you manage your infrastructure more effectively and automate the tasks that you would otherwise have to do manually. For further information, visit the product home page at `https://puppet.com/`.

Ansible	This is a simple, powerful, and easy-to-use configuration management and orchestration tool. Ansible can help you manage your infrastructure more effectively and can automate the tasks that you would otherwise have to do manually. To learn more about this IT automation technology, visit the site at `https://www.ansible.com/`.
Chef	This is a configuration management tool written in Ruby and Erlang. It uses a pure-Ruby, domain-specific language (DSL) for writing system configuration "recipes". Chef is used to streamlining the task of configuring and maintaining a company's servers and can integrate tightly with cloud-based platforms such as Amazon EC2. To explore more about this tool, visit `https://www.chef.io/`.

Microservices Architecture

The third phase of cloud-native application development is microservices architecture. This phase is all about breaking your application into small, independent services that can be deployed and scaled independently. Microservices have many benefits, such as improved scalability and resilience. However, they can also be more difficult to develop and manage. You learn more about microservices architecture in Chapter 5.

Containerization

Containerization is the process of packaging your applications into containers. Containers are a lightweight alternative to virtual machines and allow you to package your application and its dependencies. This makes it easy to deploy and run your application in any environment. There are container technologies available, such as Docker. In addition, there are several cloud-based container services, such as Amazon ECS and Google Container Engine. You learn containerization technologies in detail later in this book.

Serverless Computing

Some of the latest trends in cloud-native application development include serverless computing, which allows developers to build applications without having to worry about provisioning and managing servers.

Serverless functions are executed in response to events and are only charged for the amount of time they run. This makes them very cost-effective. There are many different serverless platforms available, such as AWS Lambda, Azure Functions, and Google Cloud Function. In addition, there are several serverless frameworks, such as Serverless Framework. You learn more about serverless computing in Chapter 5.

API Management

API management is all about designing, building, and managing APIs. An API is a set of programming instructions that allow the software to interact with other software. APIs are used to expose data and functionality to external developers. API management is a critical part of cloud-native application development. It allows you to control who has access to your API, as well as how they can use it. In addition, API management can help you monitor and troubleshoot your API. There are many API management platforms available, such as Apigee, Kong, and Amazon API Gateway. You learn more about building and deploying REST APIs later in this book.

Security

This phase is all about ensuring that your application is secure. There are many security concerns that you need to be aware of when developing a cloud-native application. These include data breaches, application vulnerabilities, and denial of service attacks. To secure your application, you need to implement security controls at every level. This includes the network, host, application, and data levels. In addition, you need to deploy security tools, such as firewalls and intrusion detection systems. There are many security products and services available, such as AWS Identity and Access Management, Azure Active Directory, and Google Cloud Identity.

DevOps Culture Shift

The cloud-native development requires a shift in culture for many organizations, from traditional waterfall development to a more agile DevOps methodology. In waterfall development, changes are made in large batches and deployed infrequently. This can lead to long development cycles and slow time-to-market. In contrast, DevOps is a more agile because it emphasizes collaboration between developers and operations teams. Changes are made in small batches and deployed frequently, which helps speed up development and improve time-to-market.

The cloud-native approach also requires changes in the way that apps are designed and built. In traditional app development, apps are typically monolithic in structure, with all components being tightly coupled. This can make it difficult to scale apps and add new features. In contrast, cloud-native apps are designed as microservices, with each component being independently deployable. This makes it easier to scale apps and add new features. It also requires changes in the way that teams are organized. In traditional app development, teams are typically siloed, with each team working in isolation. This can lead to delays and errors when teams need to coordinate their work. In contrast, cloud-native development teams are more cross-functional and collaborate closely with each other. This helps speed up development and improve the quality of the code. Overall, the cloud-native approach requires a shift in culture, methodology, and technology. It is a big change for many organizations, but the benefits are clear. Cloud-native apps are more scalable, resilient, and agile than traditional apps. They are also easier to develop and deploy.

Observability

Observability is the practice of monitoring your system in a manner where you can detect and diagnose issues as they happen. The goal of observability is to provide visibility into all aspects of your system so you can identify and fix issues before they cause customer-facing problems. This means not only monitoring system health but also tracking changes made to the system, understanding how users are interacting with it, and more. To achieve this, you must have a deep understanding of both the system and the operating environment.

It's essential to understand the difference between observability and monitoring. Monitoring is the process of collecting data about the system and using that data to generate reports. This data can be used to identify issues, but it can't be used to diagnose problems. Observability, on the other hand, allows you to detect and diagnose issues in real-time. This is because observability uses data from all levels of the system, not just the application level. There are many ways to achieve observability (see Figure 2-3), but some of the most common methods include logging, tracing, and metrics.

- **Logging:** Logging is the process of collecting and storing information about events that have occurred in the system. This data can be used to troubleshoot issues or track down problems.

- **Tracing:** Tracing is a technique that allows you to follow the path of a request as it flows through the system. This can be useful for understanding how the system works and for diagnosing problems.

- **Metrics:** Metrics are numerical values that can be used to measure various aspects of the system. You can use this data to monitor performance and identify trends.

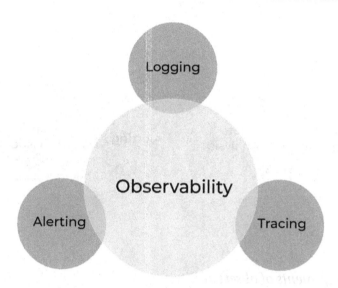

Figure 2-3. *Methods of achieving observability*

There are four critical components to observability (see Figure 2-4).

- **Collecting data:** This is typically done through logging, tracing, and metrics.

- **Analyzing data:** This involves using tools like dashboards and alerts to surface issues.

- **Alerting:** This ensures that the right people are notified when an issue arises.

- **Fixing the issue:** This is where you use the data you've collected to identify and fix the underlying problem.

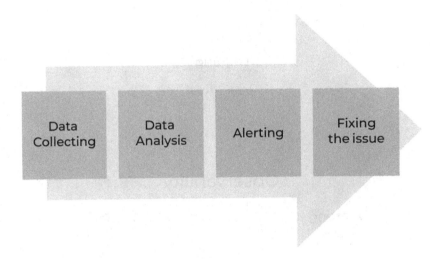

Figure 2-4. *Components of observability*

Data collection: The first step to achieving observability is data collection. You need to collect data from all the layers of the system, including the application, database, network, and infrastructure. There are many ways to collect data. Some of the most common methods include logging, tracing, and metrics.

Data analysis: The next step is data analysis. This is where you use the data you've collected to make your environment more reliable. For example, you can use data analysis for generating dashboards and reports. Dashboards are visual representations of the data that can be used to identify trends and issues. Reports are more detailed. You can use them to diagnose problems or track progress over time. You can also use them to do the following:

- Identify the root cause of problems. By tracking changes to your systems and understanding how users are interacting with them, you can quickly identify the root cause of any problems.

- Detect trends and patterns. By analyzing data over a longer period of time, you can detect trends and patterns that may not be visible when looking at data in real-time.

- Improve your monitoring coverage. By understanding which parts of your system are most important, you can focus your monitoring efforts on the areas that are most likely to cause problems.

Alerting: The next step is alerting, or sending notifications when problems are detected. This is where you ensure that the right people are notified when an issue arises. This can be done through email, SMS, or other notification systems. It's important to have a well-defined alerting strategy so that you can quickly identify and fix problems.

Best Practices for Observability

There are several best practices for achieving observability in your organization.

1. Collect data from all levels of the system—application, database, network, and infrastructure.

2. Use multiple methods of data collection—logging, tracing, and metrics—to get the most comprehensive view of the system.

3. Use short-term and long-term storage for logs. This allows you to keep track of events over a longer period of time, making it easier to identify and diagnose issues.

4. Use standardized formats. This helps you share data between different tools and systems.

5. Analyze data in real-time. Use tools like dashboards and alerts to surface issues as they happen.

6. Communicate alerts promptly. Ensure that the right people are notified when a problem arises.

7. Automate wherever possible to reduce the time and effort needed to fix problems.

This phase is about monitoring your application and gathering data about its performance. Observability is a critical part of cloud-native application development. It allows you to identify and diagnose problems with your application. In addition, observability can help you prevent problems from happening in the first place. There are many different observability tools and services available. Table 2-4 provides a list of the more popular tools.

Table 2-4. *Popular Observability Tools*

Tool	Description
New Relic	New Relic (`https://newrelic.com/`) is a SaaS-based solution that offers Application Performance Management (APM) for web and mobile applications. New Relic provides data-driven insights to help developers troubleshoot and tune their applications.
Datadog	Datadog (`www.datadoghq.com/`) is a monitoring service for cloud-based applications. It allows users to collect and visualize data from servers, databases, tools, and services to help them troubleshoot issues and identify performance bottlenecks.
AppDynamics	AppDynamics (`www.appdynamics.com/`) is an application performance monitoring (APM) solution that helps developers troubleshoot and optimize the performance of their web and mobile applications. AppDynamics provides real-time visibility into application performance so developers can identify and fix performance issues before they affect the user experience.
Splunk	Splunk (`www.splunk.com/`) is a software platform for machine data that helps developers troubleshoot, monitor, and analyze their applications. Splunk allows users to collect and index data from any source, including log files, application events, and system metrics. Splunk provides real-time visibility into application and system performance so developers can identify and fix issues before they impact the user experience.

Summary

Cloud-native applications are designed specifically to take advantage of the cloud. They have several characteristics that set them apart from traditional applications, including the following:

- They are portable and can run on any cloud platform.

- They are self-reliant and can be deployed without dependence on a specific environment or infrastructure.

- They are modular and can be broken into smaller components for easier management and scaling.

- They are elastic and can automatically scale up or down in response to changes in demand.

- They are resilient and can recover quickly from failures.

Cloud-native applications offer many benefits over traditional applications, including the following:

- **Increased agility and faster time-to-market:** Cloud-native apps can be deployed faster and with less hassle than traditional apps.

- **Lower costs:** Cloud-native apps typically require fewer resources to run, resulting in lower costs overall.

- **Improved scalability:** Cloud-native apps can scale up or down as needed, making it easier to handle fluctuations in demand.

- **Enhanced performance:** Cloud-native apps often perform better than traditional apps due to their optimized architecture.

However, there are also some drawbacks to developing cloud-native apps, including higher complexity. Cloud-native apps are more complex to develop and require more expertise. Although there are some drawbacks to developing cloud-native applications, the benefits far outweigh them in most cases. You also learned about the phases of cloud-native app development. These include continuous integration/continuous delivery (CI/CD), microservices architecture, containerization, serverless computing, API management, security, and more.

Cloud-native application development is a multi-phase process. Each phase is important and needs to be given the attention it deserves.

- **Continuous integration/continuous delivery (CI/CD):** In this phase, developers integrate code changes into a central repository and then deploy them to a test environment for verification. Changes that pass the verification process are then promoted to a production environment. This process is continuous, so new changes are always being made and tested.

- **Infrastructure as code:** In this phase, all infrastructure is defined and provisioned using code. This allows for greater flexibility and easier reproducibility of environments.

- **Microservices architecture:** In this phase, the app is broken into smaller components called microservices. Each microservice is responsible for a specific task and can be deployed independently of the others. This makes the app more scalable and resilient.

- **Containerization:** In this phase, the microservices are packaged into containers for deployment. Containers allow microservices to run on any platform without modification and make it easier to manage and scale them.

- **Serverless computing:** In this phase, the app is run in a "serverless" environment where a third party manages the servers. This eliminates the need to manage servers or infrastructure and makes it easier to scale the app as needed.

- **API management:** In this phase, the APIs that underpin the app are created and managed. This helps ensure that they are safe and secure and can be easily accessed by clients.

- **Security:** In this phase, security is implemented throughout the life of the app. This includes measures such as authentication, authorization, and data encryption.

- **DevOps culture shift:** The DevOps culture shift is necessary to enable the successful development and deployment of cloud-native applications. DevOps is all about collaboration between developers and operations staff. It helps to automate the software development process and to improve communication between teams. In addition, DevOps helps to increase the speed of delivery and to improve quality.

- **Observability (monitoring and logging):** The app's performance is monitored and logged in this phase. This helps identify issues and diagnose problems.

The cloud-native app development process is iterative, so these phases are not necessarily completed in order. However, they do represent the typical progression of a cloud-native app from initial development to production. Now that you understand the basics of cloud-native app development, you are ready to start developing your own apps. Later in this book, you put what you've learned into practice by building a cloud-native app. In the next chapter, you learn how to set up your development environment.

CHAPTER 3

Setting Up Your Development Environment

To develop cloud-native applications, you need a development environment. A development environment includes a set of tools and software you use to write, compile, test, and run your code. Setting up your development environment can seem daunting, but with the right instructions, it can be easy and straightforward. This chapter shows you how to set up your development environment for Java-based cloud-native applications. It includes detailed information about the necessary installation and configuration steps to get started with the required tools for your development environment. It covers the prerequisites and installation instructions for Java Development Kit (JDK), Maven, Git, Docker, and Kubernetes. It also discusses the benefits of using Docker and Kubernetes.

Prerequisites

The hardware requirements for developing cloud-native Java applications are very minimal. In general, most modern laptops and desktops meet the requirements. The following section lists the recommended hardware requirements for setting up your development environment.

Hardware Requirements

To develop cloud-native Java applications, you need the following hardware:

CPU: The CPU requirements for developing cloud-native Java applications are not very demanding. However, you will get better performance if you have a higher-end CPU with multiple cores.

© Tarun Telang 2023
T. Telang, *Beginning Cloud Native Development with MicroProfile, Jakarta EE, and Kubernetes*,
https://doi.org/10.1007/978-1-4842-8832-0_3

Memory: 4GB of RAM or more

Hard drive space: At least 50GB of free disk space

Operating Systems

The operating system requirements for developing cloud-native Java applications are also modest. You can use any of the following operating systems:

- Windows 10 or later

- macOS 10.13 or higher

- Linux: Ubuntu 18.04 or higher, Fedora 28 or higher

If you are not sure about the system architecture of your computer, you can use the following commands to determine it.

In a Linux or MacOS, you can find your system architecture by running the following command:

```
uname -m
```

The output of this command will show the architecture of your system. For example, on a 64-bit system, you see the following output:

```
x86_64
```

For Windows, use the following command:

```
echo %PROCESSOR_ARCHITECTURE%
```

Software Dependencies

In addition to the hardware requirements, you need to install a few software dependencies before you can start developing cloud-native Java applications. These dependencies include the following:

- **JDK 17 or later:** You can download the latest JDK from the Oracle website (`www.oracle.com/java/technologies/downloads/`).

- **Maven:** You can download Maven from the Apache Maven website (`https://maven.apache.org/`).

- **Git:** You can download Git from the Git website (`https://git-scm.com/`).

- **GitHub account:** If you do not have one, you can create a free account on the GitHub website (`https://github.com/`).

- **Docker:** You must download the Docker Desktop for Mac or Windows.

- **Docker Hub account:** You need an account on the Docker Hub website. You can create one at the Docker Hub website (`https://hub.docker.com/`), if you don't already one.

Installing Java Development Kit (JDK)

Java Development Kit (JDK) is a software development environment used to develop Java applications. It includes the Java Runtime Environment (JRE), which is required to run Java applications, and the Java compiler, which is used to compile Java source code into bytecode.

Before installing the JDK, you need to check if you already have it installed on your system. To do this, open a terminal window and type the following command:

```
java -version
```

If the JDK is installed on your system, you should see something like the following output:

```
java version "17.0.1" 2021-10-19 LTS
Java(TM) SE Runtime Environment (build 17.0.1+12-LTS-jvmci-21.3-b05)
Java HotSpot(TM) 64-Bit Server VM (build 17.0.1+12-LTS-jvmci-21.3-b05,
mixed mode, sharing)
```

If you see this output, this means the JDK is already installed on your system and you can skip to the next section.

If you do not have the JDK installed on your system, follow these steps to install the JDK:

1. Download JDK 17 or later from the Oracle website (`https://www.oracle.com/java/technologies/downloads/`).

2. Once you have downloaded the JDK, run the downloaded installer and follow the on-screen instructions to complete the installation.

The JAVA_HOME environment variable is used by Java applications to determine the location of the JDK installation. It is important to set this variable correctly to ensure that your Java applications will run properly.

The Oracle JDK installer for Windows will automatically set the JAVA_HOME environment variable for you. If you use a different JDK, such as OpenJDK, you need to manually set the JAVA_HOME environment variable. OpenJDK (Open Java Development Kit) is a free and open-source implementation of the Java Platform, Standard Edition (Java SE). You can find more details about OpenJDK on its project website at openjdk.org.

To set the JAVA_HOME environment variable, open a terminal window and type the following command:

```
export JAVA_HOME=<path-to-jdk>
```

Where <path-to-jdk> is the location of your JDK installation. For example, if you installed the JDK in /usr/local/jdk, you would type the following command:

```
export JAVA_HOME=/usr/local/jdk
```

You can verify that the JAVA_HOME variable is set correctly by typing the following command:

```
echo $JAVA_HOME
```

If the Java_HOME variable is set correctly, you should see the location of your JDK installation. For example:

```
/usr/local/jdk
```

Once the installation is complete, verify the installation by running the java -version command.

If you see the version printed, it means that the JDK has been successfully installed on your system.

Using Maven

Maven is a build automation tool used for Java applications. It manages dependencies, compiles code, runs tests, and packages code into deployable artifacts. Maven is required to build cloud-native Java applications. Appendix A explains Maven in detail.

Installing Maven

To install Maven on your system, follow these steps:

1. Download the latest version of Maven from the Apache Maven website (`https://maven.apache.org/`).

2. Extract the downloaded archive to the directory of your choice.

3. Add the `bin` directory of the extracted Maven folder to your PATH environment variable.

4. Verify the installation by running the following command:

   ```
   mvn -v
   ```

You should see output similar to the following:

```
Apache Maven 3.8.5 (3599d3414f046de2324203b78ddcf9b5e4388aa0)
Maven home: /Users/home/apache-maven-3.8.5
Java version: 17.0.1, vendor: Oracle Corporation, runtime: /Library/Java/
JavaVirtualMachines/jdk17.0_1.jdk/Contents/Home/jre
Default locale: en_IN, platform encoding: UTF-8
OS name: "mac os x", version: "11.5.1", arch: "x86_64", family: "mac"
```

If you see the output as in Figure 3-1, it means that Maven has been successfully installed on your system.

```
● ● ●              grpc_demo — root@2046c5dccbd0: / — -zsh — 78×22
$ mvn -v
Apache Maven 3.8.6 (84538c9988a25aec085021c365c560670ad80f63)
Maven home: /opt/homebrew/Cellar/maven/3.8.6/libexec
Java version: 17.0.1, vendor: Oracle Corporation, runtime: /Library/Java/JavaV
irtualMachines/graalvm-ee-java17-21.3.0/Contents/Home
Default locale: en_IN, platform encoding: UTF-8
OS name: "mac os x", version: "11.5.1", arch: "x86_64", family: "mac"
$
```

Figure 3-1. *The output of the mvn -v command*

See Appendix B to learn how to create a Jakarta EE web app project using Maven.

Git

Git is a distributed version control system used to track changes in software development projects.

Installing Git

To install Git on your system, follow these steps:

1. Download the latest version of Git from the Git website (`https://git-scm.com/`). Figure 3-2 shows the home page of the Git website.

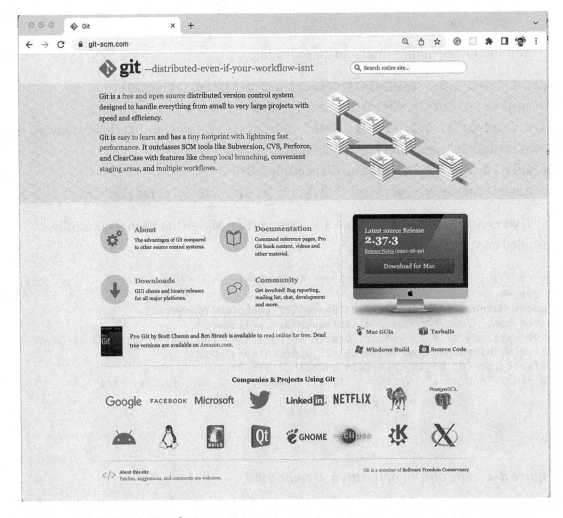

Figure 3-2. *The git-scm home page*

2. Run the downloaded installer and follow the on-screen instructions to complete the installation.

3. Verify the installation by running the following command:

   ```
   git --version
   ```

You should see output similar to the following:

```
git version 2.31.1
```

Creating a GitHub Account

GitHub is a code-hosting platform for version control and collaboration. It is used to store the code for this example application. If you don't have a GitHub account, create one by following these steps:

1. Go to the GitHub website (`https://github.com/`) and click the Sign up button.

2. Enter your email address, password, and username in the respective fields.

3. You are asked whether you would like to receive product updates and announcements via emails. Select "y" for yes or "n" for no based on your preference.

4. After verifying the CAPTCHA, click the Create Account button.

5. Then enter a verification code that you received in your email provided in the previous step.

6. After validating the code, you can click Skip Personalization to navigate directly to your GitHub Dashboard.

You are now all set for using GitHub.

Creating a GitHub Repository

In this section, you learn how to create a GitHub repository for your project.

1. Log in to your GitHub account and click the + icon at the top-right corner of the page.

2. On the next page, click New Repository.

3. On the Create a New Repository page, enter the following details (see Figure 3-3 for reference):

   - **Owner:** Ensure you select your GitHub username. This should be selected by default.

   - **Repository name:** Choose cloud-native-app in this case.

   - **Description (optional):** A Java-based cloud-native application development project.

   - **Public/private:** Choose Public if you want anyone on the Internet to see this repository.

   - **Initialize this repository with:** Select the Add a README file checkbox. It's good practice to add a README file to your project repositories. This file contains information about the project, such as what the project is about, how to set it up, and so on.

   - **Add .gitignore:** Choose Java for the .gitignore template.

   - **License:** None.

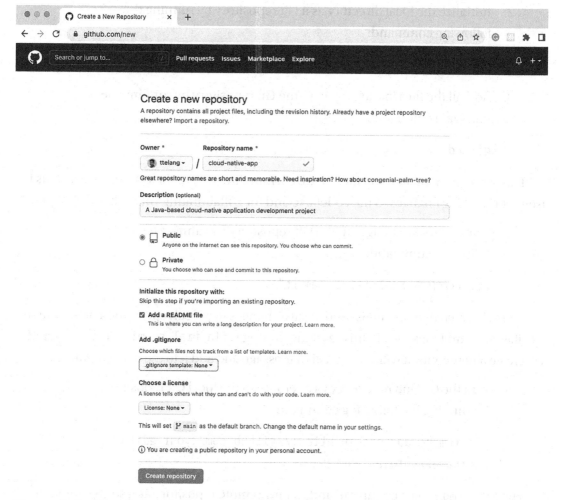

Figure 3-3. *The Create Repository page in GitHub*

4. Click the Create Repository button. Your GitHub repository for the project should now be complete.

Pushing Code to a GitHub Repository

In this section, you learn how to push your project code to a GitHub repository.

1. Open a terminal window and change the current working directory to the location of your project.

2. Initialize the local directory as a Git repository by running the
    following command:

    ```
    git init
    ```

3. Add all the files in the project to the Git repository by running the
    following command:

    ```
    git add .
    ```

This `git` command adds all files in the current directory to the Git repository. This is useful for tracking changes to the codebase and for collaborating with other developers.

4. Commit these changes to the Git repository by running the
    following command:

    ```
    git commit -m "Initial commit"
    ```

The `git commit` command is used to save changes to a local repository. The -m option specifies a commit message. In this case, the message is `Initial commit`. This command will create a new commit with the specified message and add it to the current branch.

5. Add the GitHub repository as a remote to the local Git repository
    by running the following command:

    ```
    git remote add origin https://github.com/<your-github-
    username>/<project-name>.git
    ```

The `git remote add` command adds a new remote repository as a source for your local repository. In this case, you are adding the project hosted on GitHub as the origin for your local repository. Replace the `<your-github-username>` and `<project-name>` variables with your actual GitHub username and project name.

6. Push the changes to the GitHub repository by running the
    following command:

    ```
    git push -u origin <branch-name>
    ```

This `git` command is used to push your code to the server. The -u option is used to set the upstream repository, which is the remote repository your local repository will be pushing to. The `origin` is the name of the remote repository; replace <branch-name> with the name of the branch that you want to push your code into, such as `master`.

You should see the following output:

```
Enumerating objects: 40, done.
Counting objects: 100% (40/40), done.
Delta compression using up to 8 threads
Compressing objects: 100% (31/31), done.
Writing objects: 100% (40/40), 63.79 KiB | 21.26 MiB/s, done.
Total 40 (delta 3), reused 0 (delta 0), pack-reused 0
remote: Resolving deltas: 100% (3/3), done.
remote:
remote: Create a pull request for 'master' on GitHub by visiting:
remote:        https://github.com/ttelang/cloud-native-app/pull/new/master
remote:
To https://github.com/ttelang/cloud-native-app.git
 * [new branch]        master -> master
```

Your project has now been pushed to the GitHub repository.

Using Docker

Almost all applications these days are leveraging containers in one way or another. Docker is a containerization platform used for packaging and running a complete application environment into small, isolated, and portable containers. Using the Docker platform, you can easily configure and customize containers to run various operating systems, web servers, application servers, databases, and so on. Docker makes it very easy for developers to package an application with all of the libraries and dependencies, and ship it out as one single, lightweight package. This package can then be deployed to a container and can be ported to various cloud environments.

Benefits of Using Docker

Docker containers are a lightweight alternative to virtual machines that can provide many benefits for application development, including:

- **Isolation:** Containers isolate applications from each other and the underlying infrastructure. This isolation can increase security and improve reproducibility between development, test, and production environments.

- **Portability:** Containers can be deployed on any host with a supported container runtime, making it easy to move applications among development, test, and production environments.

- **Efficiency:** Containers use far less disk space and memory than virtual machines, so they can be run on smaller, less powerful hosts. In addition, multiple containers can be run on a single host, further increasing efficiency.

- **Flexibility:** Containers can be deployed in a wide variety of environments, from on-premises data centers to public clouds.

Docker containers are often used in conjunction with Kubernetes, a container orchestration platform that provides additional features and functionality for managing containers at scale.

Installing Docker

In this section, you learn how to install and set up Docker on your system. To install Docker on your system, follow these steps:

1. Download Docker Desktop for Mac or Windows from the Docker website (`https://www.docker.com/`).

2. Run the downloaded installer and follow the on-screen instructions to complete the installation.

3. Verify the installation by running the following command:

   ```
   docker --version
   ```

You should see output similar to the following:

```
Docker version 20.10.11, build dea9396
```

If you see this output, it means that Docker has been successfully installed on your system.

Docker installation may not be straightforward, depending on your system configuration. If you have any problems installing Docker, consult the documentation (`https://docs.docker.com/install/`) for more information.

Docker Hub

Docker Hub is a public registry that contains a large number of Docker images that can be used for various purposes. For example, you can find a MongoDB image, or a Tomcat image, or a Java application server image on Docker Hub. You can also create your images and push them to the public registry so that others can use them.

Creating a Docker Hub Account

If you don't have a Docker Hub account, create one by following these steps:

1. Go to the Docker website (`https://hub.docker.com/`) and click the Register button.

2. On the Sign Up page (Figure 3-4), enter your username, email address, and password.

3. Click the checkbox to Agree to the Service Agreements, Privacy Policies & Data Processing Terms.

4. Verify the reCAPTCHA and click the Sign Up button to create your Docker Hub account.

5. Now you can log in to the Docker Hub website to access the library of container images.

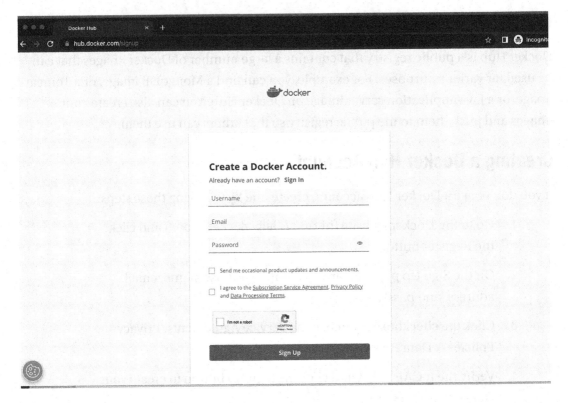

Figure 3-4. *Docker Hub sign up page*

Once you have successfully created both GitHub and Docker Hub accounts, you are ready to set up your development environment for Java-based cloud-native application development. In Chapter 9, you learn how to create a Docker image and push it to Docker Hub.

Using Kubernetes

Kubernetes is a powerful tool that can help you automate the deployment and scaling of your containerized applications. As Kubernetes requires Docker to be configured correctly, it is important to understand the benefits of using both technologies together. Kubernetes provides several benefits, such as automated deployment and scaling of containerized applications, self-healing capabilities, service discovery and load balancing, and storage orchestration.

Kubernetes is an open-source container orchestration platform that automates the deployment, scaling, and management of containerized applications. In this section, you install Kubernetes on your development machine. The easiest way to install Kubernetes is by using a tool, such as Minikube. Minikube is a single-node Kubernetes cluster that runs on your development machine. Minikube provides several benefits, including:

- It is easy to install and get started.

- It can run locally on your development machine.

- There is no need to provision or manage any infrastructure for running Minikube.

You learn more about Kubernetes and container orchestration in Chapter 9.

Installing Kubernetes

To install Minikube, follow the instructions on the "Get Started" section of the Minikube documentation website (https://minikube.sigs.k8s.io/docs/start/).

You need to run the appropriate installation command as per your platform architecture and operation system.

On Windows, you can download and run the latest installer using this link: https://storage.googleapis.com/minikube/releases/latest/minikube-installer.exe.

On macOS or Linux, you need to run the curl command, as shown here:

```
curl -LO https://storage.googleapis.com/minikube/releases/latest/minikube-<operating system>-<architecture>
sudo install minikube-<operating system> -<architecture> /usr/local/bin/minikube
```

Be sure to replace <architecture> with x86-64 or arm64 and <operation system> with linux for Linux operating system or darwin for macOS. You are prompted to enter your administration or root password for the system.

This will install the latest Minikube stable release using the binary download.

Now start the Docker service on your machine and verify the installation by running the following command:

```
minikube start
```

You should see output similar to the following:

```
$ minikube start
😄 minikube v1.25.2 on Darwin 11.5.1 (arm64)
✨ Using the docker driver based on existing profile
👍 Starting control plane node minikube in cluster minikube
🚜 Pulling base image ...
🔥 Creating docker container (CPUs=2, Memory=1988MB) ...
🐳 Preparing Kubernetes v1.23.3 on Docker 20.10.12 ...
    ▪ kubelet.housekeeping-interval=5m
    ▪ Generating certificates and keys ...
    ▪ Booting up control plane ...
    ▪ Configuring RBAC rules ...
🔎 Verifying Kubernetes components...
    ▪ Using image gcr.io/k8s-minikube/storage-provisioner:v5
🌟 Enabled addons: storage-provisioner, default-storageclass
🏄 Done! kubectl is now configured to use "minikube" cluster and "default" namespace by
default
```

If you see the output shown in Figure 3-5, that means that Minikube has been successfully installed on your system.

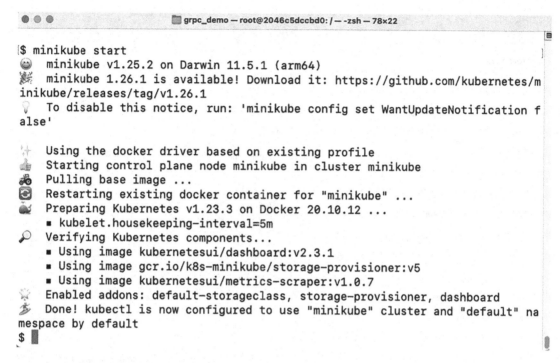

Figure 3-5. *The output of the Minikube start command*

Configuring Docker for Kubernetes

Minikube is a great way to get started with Kubernetes, as it is easy to install and get started with. By configuring Docker to use the correct settings, you can ensure that your applications will run correctly on Kubernetes. To configure Docker for Kubernetes on Windows, follow these instructions:

1. Right-click the Docker icon in the system tray and select Settings.

2. Select Kubernetes and check the Enable Kubernetes checkbox.

3. Click Apply & Restart.

To configure Docker for Kubernetes on macOS, follow these instructions:

1. Open the Docker Desktop preferences window.

2. Click the Kubernetes tab.

3. Select Enable Kubernetes, as shown in Figure 3-6.

4. Click Apply & Restart. This will restart Docker and enable Kubernetes.

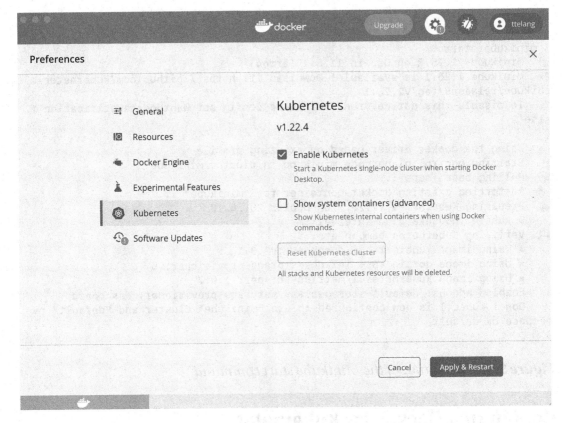

Figure 3-6. *Kubernetes preferences in Docker Desktop*

To configure Docker for Kubernetes on Linux, follow these instructions:

1. Open the Docker daemon configuration file in a text editor. The
   file is located at /etc/docker/daemon.json.

2. Add the following lines to the file:

```
{
"exec-opts": ["native.cgroupdriver=systemd"],
"log-driver": "json-file",
"log-opts": {
"max-size": "100m"
},
"storage-driver": "overlay2"
}
```

3. Save the file and exit the text editor.

4. Restart the Docker daemon.

5. To verify that Kubernetes is enabled, run the following command:

```
docker info | grep -i "kubernetes"
```

You should see the following output:

```
WARNING: No swap limit support
Kubernetes Root Dir: /var/lib/kubelet
Kubernetes Runtime Wants Filesystem: true
Kubernetes Runtime Execs Mounted via Containerd: false
Runtimes: docker runc
Default RuntimeName: docker

Init binary path: /usr/local/bin/podman
Kubernetes version: v1.15.3
Cgroup Driver: systemd
```

Creating a Kubernetes Cluster

A Kubernetes cluster is a set of nodes or servers used to run containerized applications. Each node in a Kubernetes cluster runs a Kubernetes agent, which manages the applications running on that node. The agent communicates with a Kubernetes master, which is responsible for managing the entire cluster.

In this section, you create a Kubernetes cluster using Minikube.

1. If Minikube is not already running, start it by running the following command:

```
$ minikube start
```

2. Verify that the cluster is up and running by running the following command:

```
$ kubectl get nodes
```

3. You should see the following output:

```
$ kubectl get po -A
```

NAMESPACE	NAME		READY	STATUS
RESTARTS		AGE		
kube-system	coredns-64897985d-h2cwq		1/1	Running
0		2m		
kube-system	etcd-minikube		1/1	Running
0		2m15s		
kube-system	kube-apiserver-minikube		1/1	Running
0		2m15s		
kube-system	kube-controller-manager-minikube		1/1	Running
0		2m13s		
kube-system	kube-proxy-wm5c5		1/1	Running
0		2m		
kube-system	kube-scheduler-minikube		1/1	Running
0		2m14s		
kube-system	storage-provisioner		1/1	Running
1 (89s ago)		2m12s		

Using Zipkin

Zipkin is a distributed tracing system. It helps you to understand how your application is behaving and provides insights into the performance of individual microservices.

Installing Zipkin

To install Zipkin, you first need to install Java. Once Java is installed, you can download and install Zipkin from the following link:

https://zipkin.io/pages/quickstart

Once Zipkin is installed, you can start it by running the following command:

```
java -jar zipkin.jar
```

Zipkin will then start up and be available at http://localhost:9411/. You can access the Zipkin UI to view trace data, as shown in Figure 3-7.

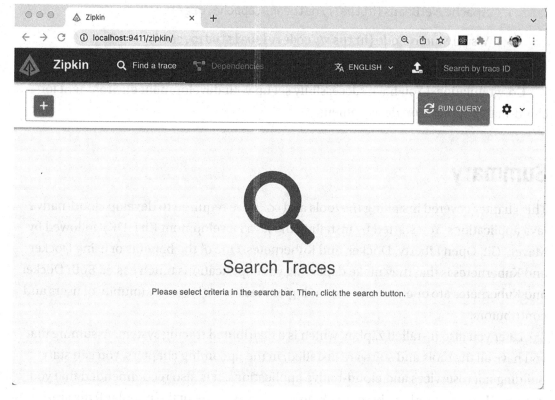

Figure 3-7. *Zipkin UI to view traces*

Integrated Development Environments (IDE)

An IDE, or Integrated Development Environment, is a software tool used for developing software applications. It includes features for editing code, compiling code, running tests, and debugging applications. Some popular IDEs include Eclipse, IntelliJ, Visual Studio Code, and Apache NetBeans.

Before you begin, you need to have an Integrated Development Environment (IDE) of your choice. Some popular IDEs for Java development are

- IntelliJ IDEA Ultimate or Community Edition (`www.jetbrains. com/idea/`)

- Eclipse IDE for Enterprise Java and Web Developers (`www.eclipse. org/downloads/packages/`)

- Apache NetBeans (`https://netbeans.apache.org/`)

- Visual Studio Code (`https://code.visualstudio.com/`)

Or any other IDE of your choice.

Congratulations! You have successfully set up your development environment for cloud-native application development.

Summary

This chapter covered installing the tools and software required to develop cloud-native Java applications. You started by installing the Java Development Kit (JDK), followed by Maven, Git, Open Liberty, Docker, and Kubernetes. One of the benefits of using Docker and Kubernetes is that they make deploying your applications much easier. Both Docker and Kubernetes are open-source technologies that have a large community of users and contributors.

Later you also installed Zipkin, which is a distributed tracing system. Assuming that you have all the tools and software installed, in the upcoming chapters, you can start building microservices and cloud-native applications. It is also recommended that you use an IDE, as it provides a better coding experience. Some of the popular IDEs are Eclipse, IntelliJ IDEA, NetBeans, and Visual Studio Code.

CHAPTER 4

Building RESTful Web Services

In Chapter 2, you learned that microservices is an architectural style that structures an application as a collection of small, modular services. Microservices are independently deployable, scalable, and testable services that communicate with each other through well-defined APIs. This decoupling of services promotes development and deployment agility, as well as operational resilience.

RESTful API is an application programming interface (API) that conforms to the constraints of the REST architectural style and allows for interaction with RESTful web services. For example, Facebook, Twitter, and Google offer their functionality as RESTful web services that any client application can use to call these web services via REST.

The three key components of a RESTful API are:

- The client that runs on a user's computer or smartphone and initiates communication

- The server offering an API as a means to access its data or features

- The resource, which is any piece of content that the server can provide to the client

When a client requests a resource via a RESTful API, the server transmits a representation (via HTTP/JSON) of the resource's state to the requestor or endpoint.

In this chapter, you learn how to create a RESTful web service using the Jakarta EE platform. You also learn how to deploy and test your web service on an Open Liberty server. First, the chapter focuses on creating a server-side component using the Jakarta RESTful Web Service (formerly JAX-RS). You will start by creating a simple web service that returns basic information about products. Then you will add more functionality, such as returning a list of products and allowing the client to create a new product.

© Tarun Telang 2023
T. Telang, *Beginning Cloud Native Development with MicroProfile, Jakarta EE, and Kubernetes*,
https://doi.org/10.1007/978-1-4842-8832-0_4

REST: An Architectural Style for Building Web Services

Representational State Transfer (REST) is an architectural style that defines a set of constraints for creating web services. Web services that conform to the REST architectural style, or simply RESTful web services, provide interoperability between computer systems on the Internet. REST-compliant web services allow the requesting systems to access and manipulate textual representations of web resources by using a uniform and predefined set of stateless operations. The REST style uses standard HTTP methods (such as GET, POST, PUT, and DELETE) to manipulate resources. It also uses simple URL syntax to access resources, and it uses standard HTTP status codes to indicate the result of a request.

The REST architectural style defines a set of constraints that must be followed to create a RESTful API. The key constraints are as follows:

- Clients should be able to access resources using standard HTTP methods (GET, POST, PUT, DELETE).

- Clients should be able to determine the URI for each resource.

- Resources should be represented in JSON or XML format.

- Server should return the correct HTTP response code (200 OK, 404 Not Found, and so on) for each request.

Introduction to Open Liberty Runtime

Open Liberty (https://openliberty.io/) is a flexible and open-source server runtime environment that enables you to build and deploy microservices-based applications rapidly. It is a lightweight, modular runtime environment with a fast start up and a low memory footprint. It provides the foundation you need to build microservices apps quickly and efficiently.

The IBM WebSphere Liberty application server (www.ibm.com/in-en/cloud/websphere-liberty) is built on Open Liberty. Open Liberty is a flexible runtime environment that supports multiple programming models, languages, and frameworks. You can use the technology of your choice with Open Liberty, without worrying about lock-in. Open Liberty is backed by a large and vibrant open-source community.

Key Features of the Open Liberty Application Server

Open Liberty provides a set of features specifically targeted at enhancing the development, deployment, and management of microservices apps. It offers the following key features that help you develop, deploy, and manage microservices-based applications:

- **Rapid development of microservices:** Open Liberty lets you quickly develop microservices-based applications using your favorite IDEs, such as Eclipse or IntelliJ IDEA. You can also use any build tool, such as Maven or Gradle.

- **Easy deployment to different environments:** Open Liberty provides you with multiple deployment options so that you can deploy your application to the platform of your choice. You can also use a container technology, such as Docker.

- **Remote administration, monitoring, and management:** Open Liberty provides you with various management options, so you can manage your application in the way that best suits your needs. It provides built-in support for monitoring and managing your application. You can use the Open Liberty Admin Center, which is a graphical user interface to monitor your application's health and performance. It also provides the Open Liberty command-line interface for a more scripted approach.

- **Cloud-ready:** Open Liberty is designed for the cloud. It supports the latest standards and technologies, including Jakarta EE and Eclipse MicroProfile.

- **Support for Java standards and technologies:** Open Liberty supports all the features in MicroProfile, as well as many features from the Jakarta EE specification. This means that you can write Jakarta EE applications and deploy them on Open Liberty.

- **Security:** Open Liberty provides comprehensive security features, including support for Single Sign-On (SSO) and Transport Layer Security (TLS). TLS provides a secure connection between the client and server, while SSO allows users to log in once and access all the applications they are authorized to use. These features make Open Liberty an ideal choice for organizations that must ensure the security of their web applications and data.

Downloading and Installing Open Liberty

Installing Open Liberty is a simple process and only takes a few minutes. Here are the steps for Installing Open Liberty on your computer:

1. Download Open Liberty from `https://openliberty.io/ downloads/`.

2. To install Open Liberty, extract the contents of the downloaded file into the directory of your choice.

The folder structure of the extracted content should be as follows:

```
wlp
├── BETA_NOTICES
├── LICENSE
├── README.TXT
├── bin
├── clients
├── dev
├── lib
├── templates
└── usr
```

You can use Open Liberty to develop applications that are designed for the cloud and that can be deployed in a microservices architecture.

Starting the Open Liberty Server

Once you have extracted the contents of the downloaded file, you can start Open Liberty by running the following command from the `bin` folder:

```
$ ./server start
```

You will then see the output shown in Figure 4-1.

Figure 4-1. Output of the ./server start command

You can set the PATH environment variable so that you can start the server from any directory and without prefixing the command with ./. as per the following steps.

For Linux or macOS:

- Based on your current shell, open the .bash_profile or .zshrc file of your home directory in a text editor. If you don't have this file, create one in your home directory.

- Add the following line to the file:

export PATH=<path-to-directory>;$PATH

For Windows:

- If you are using Windows you can the full path using the following command or by setting the environment variables in the Control Panel ➤ Advanced System Settings area:

set PATH=<path-to-directory>;%PATH%

Replace <path-to-directory> with the path where the server executable file is located. You should restart the command prompt or your terminal to accept your changes.

This will start an instance of Open Liberty with the default configuration. You can then access this instance at the following URL: http://localhost:9080/. Figure 4-2 shows the welcome page of the Open Liberty server.

Figure 4-2. *Open Liberty welcome page*

This verifies that Open Liberty is installed successfully. You are now ready to create your first application.

Printing a List of Features on the Open Liberty Server

You can print the list of features installed on your Open Liberty server using the productInfo command. This is a useful command to see what features are installed and running.

To print the list of installed features, you simply need to open a terminal and run this command:

```
./productInfo featureInfo
```

Figure 4-3 shows the output.

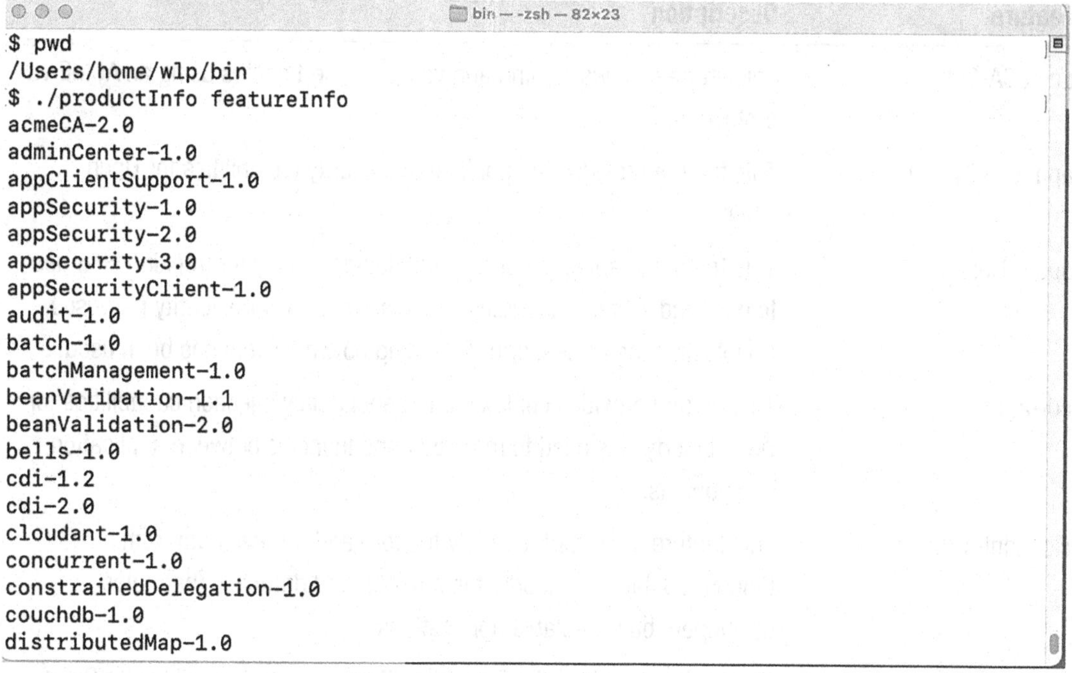

```
$ pwd
/Users/home/wlp/bin
$ ./productInfo featureInfo
acmeCA-2.0
adminCenter-1.0
appClientSupport-1.0
appSecurity-1.0
appSecurity-2.0
appSecurity-3.0
appSecurityClient-1.0
audit-1.0
batch-1.0
batchManagement-1.0
beanValidation-1.1
beanValidation-2.0
bells-1.0
cdi-1.2
cdi-2.0
cloudant-1.0
concurrent-1.0
constrainedDelegation-1.0
couchdb-1.0
distributedMap-1.0
```

Figure 4-3. *The output of the ./productInfo featureInfo stop command*

There are a large number of features supported by the Open Liberty server.
Table 4-1 provides a list of the first few features supported by the Open Liberty server, to
demonstrate how extensible and modular the Open Liberty Server is.

Table 4-1. *Open Liberty Features and Descriptions*

Feature	Description
acmeCA-2.0:	This feature allows signing and validating certificates using an ACME v2 protocol.
appSecurity-3.0:	This feature provides the application security capabilities for Open Liberty.
audit-1.0:	This feature enables the auditing of server activity for tracking changes to data and system resources. This can be used for security purposes, troubleshooting issues, or determining how a system has been used.
cdi-2.0:	This feature provides contexts and dependency injection capabilities for Open Liberty. It is used to manage dependencies between application components.
cloudant-1.0:	This feature provides the ability to store and retrieve data from a Cloudant database. Cloudant is a distributed database that helps developers build scalable applications.
concurrent-1.0:	This feature provides the Enterprise Concurrency Utilities 1.0 for Open Liberty.
constrainedDelegation-1.0:	This feature allows for delegation of constrained resources between servers. This can be used to improve security or to allow for easier management of delegated resources.
couchdb-1.0:	This feature provides the ability to store and retrieve data from a CouchDB database. CouchDB is a document-oriented database that helps developers build scalable applications.
distributedMap-1.0:	This feature provides a distributed map that can be used to share data between servers.

For a complete list of features, visit the official documentation page at `www.ibm.com/docs/en/was-liberty/base?topic=management-liberty-features`.

Creating a Server Instance

You might need a new server instance if you want to run a different set of features or want to further optimize performance. Creating a new server instance is simple. You just need to use the `server create` command followed by the name of the new server. In this case, call the new server `my-server`.

```
./server create my-server
```

The output of this command is shown in Figure 4-4.

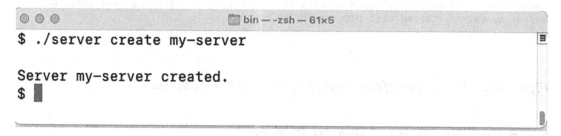

Figure 4-4. *The output of the ./server create my-server command*

It creates a new directory called `my-server`, which contains all the files needed to run your new server instance. Figure 4-5 shows the newly created directory.

Figure 4-5. *Folder structure of the new server instance of Open Liberty*

Different folders are used to store different types of files in the Open Liberty server. The `apps` folder stores applications that you want to run on your server. The `dropins` folder stores files you want to add to your server instance. The `workarea` folder stores temporary files that are used by the server.

Open Liberty provides a simple way to deploy applications to your server. You can just move the deployable file into the `dropins` folder inside the server directory. Open Liberty will automatically deploy the application and restart the server if required.

You can start your new server instance using the server start command, as follows:

```
./server start my-server
```

The output of this command is shown in Figure 4-6.

Figure 4-6. *The output of the ./server start my-server command*

Stopping the Open Liberty Server

If you want to stop your newly created server instance, you can use the server stop command, followed by the server's name. For example, consider this command:

```
./server stop my-server
```

It gives the output shown in Figure 4-7.

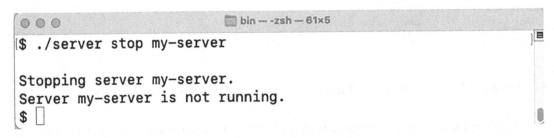

Figure 4-7. *The output of the ./server stop my-server command*

To stop the default instance of Open Liberty that you started, you can run the following command:

```
./server stop
```

Once the command executes successfully, you'll see the output in Figure 4-8.

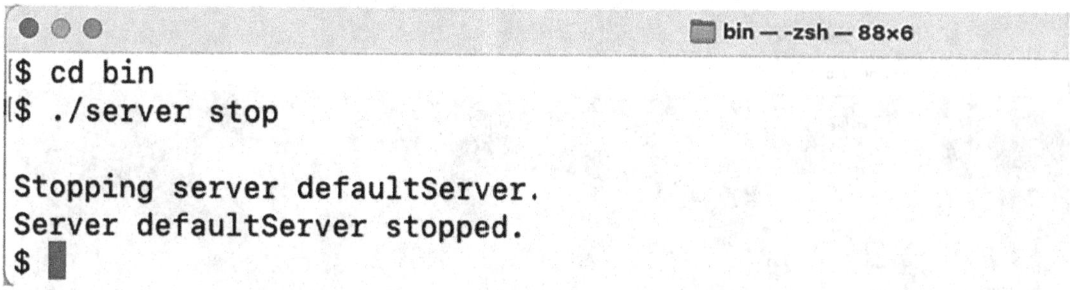

```
● ● ●                                          📁 bin — -zsh — 88×6
$ cd bin
$ ./server stop

Stopping server defaultServer.
Server defaultServer stopped.
$ ▊
```

Figure 4-8. *The output of the ./server stop command*

Configuring the Server

You can configure your server using a configuration file called `server.xml`. You can also add features to your server by adding the `featureManager` element to your `server.xml` file. For example, you can add the `restfulWS-3.0` and `jsonb-2.0` features by adding the following XML:

```
<featureManager>
    <feature>restfulWS-3.0</feature>
    <feature>jsonb-2.0</feature>
</featureManager>
```

Open Liberty is aware of its required dependencies, and it will take care of adding them. If you want to disable a feature, simply remove the `feature` element from your `server.xml` file.

Creating a RESTful Web Service in Open Liberty

If you are starting from scratch, you can get started quickly by utilizing starter applications that are created using the Get Started - Open Liberty website at `https://openliberty.io/start`. You will see the form in Figure 4-9.

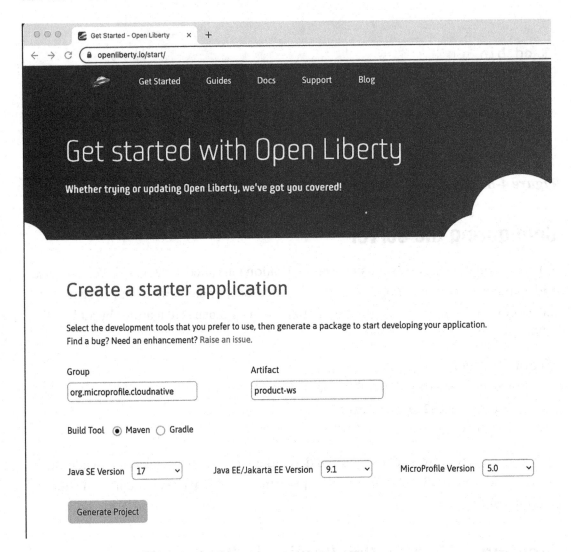

Figure 4-9. *The Get Started - Open Liberty web page*

You need to provide the following details:

Group ID: org.microprofile.cloudnative

Artifact ID: product-ws

Build Tool: Maven

Java SE Version: 17

Java EE/Jakarta EE Version: 9.1

MicroProfile Version: 5.0

Choose the desired build tool. Maven and Gradle are both supported. This book uses Maven; if you want to, you can easily migrate to Gradle later. This example uses Java SE Version 17 and MicroProfile Version 5.0, as these were the latest stable versions supported by Open Liberty at the time of this writing. When you're ready, click the Generate Project button to download the generated project.

Exploring the Project Structure

You can unzip the project. Its structure should look like this:

```
product-ws
├── Dockerfile
├── README.txt
├── mvnw
├── mvnw.cmd
├── pom.xml
└── src
    └── main
        ├── java
        │   └── org
        │       └── microprofile
        │           └── rest
        │               └── RestApplication.java
        └── liberty
            └── config
                └── server.xml
```

Dockerfile can be used to build and run the application in a Docker container (which is covered in Chapter 9). The mvnw and mvnw.cmd scripts can be used to build and run the application without installing Maven.

Understanding the Maven pom.xml File for the Open Liberty Project

The Open Liberty starter provides you with a simple and quick method to obtain the files you need to begin developing an application in Open Liberty. When you use the Open Liberty starter to generate your project, a pom.xml file includes dependencies for the latest stable versions of Open Liberty features. The liberty-maven-plugin file is also included so that you can deploy and run your application on an Open Liberty server. Here is the source code contained in the pom.xml file:

```xml
<?xml version="1.0" encoding="UTF-8" ?>
<project xmlns="http://maven.apache.org/POM/4.0.0"
  xmlns:xsi="http://www.w3.org/2001/XMLSchema-instance"
  xsi:schemaLocation="http://maven.apache.org/POM/4.0.0 http://maven.
apache.org/xsd/maven-4.0.0.xsd">
  <modelVersion>4.0.0</modelVersion>

  <groupId>org.microprofile.cloudnative</groupId>
  <artifactId>product-ws</artifactId>
  <version>1.0-SNAPSHOT</version>
  <packaging>war</packaging>

  <properties>
    <maven.compiler.source>17</maven.compiler.source>
    <maven.compiler.target>17</maven.compiler.target>
    <project.build.sourceEncoding>UTF-8</project.build.sourceEncoding>
  </properties>

  <dependencies>
    <dependency>
      <groupId>jakarta.platform</groupId>
      <artifactId>jakarta.jakartaee-api</artifactId>
      <version>9.1.0</version>
      <scope>provided</scope>
    </dependency>
    <dependency>
      <groupId>org.eclipse.microprofile</groupId>
      <artifactId>microprofile</artifactId>
      <version>5.0</version>
      <type>pom</type>
      <scope>provided</scope>
    </dependency>
  </dependencies>
```

```
<build>
  <finalName>product-ws</finalName>
  <pluginManagement>
    <plugins>
      <plugin>
        <groupId>org.apache.maven.plugins</groupId>
        <artifactId>maven-war-plugin</artifactId>
        <version>3.3.2</version>
      </plugin>
      <plugin>
        <groupId>io.openliberty.tools</groupId>
        <artifactId>liberty-maven-plugin</artifactId>
        <version>3.5.2</version>
      </plugin>
    </plugins>
  </pluginManagement>
  <plugins>
    <plugin>
      <groupId>io.openliberty.tools</groupId>
      <artifactId>liberty-maven-plugin</artifactId>
    </plugin>
  </plugins>
</build>
</project>
```

Explanation:

- Line 1: The XML declaration defines the XML version (1.0) and the encoding (UTF-8).

- Line 2: The project element is the *root* of the POM. All other elements must be nested inside this element.

- Lines 3-4: The xmlns attribute defines the XML namespaces used by Maven. The xsi:schemaLocation attribute defines the location of the schema used to validate the POM.

- Line 5: The modelVersion element defines the version of the POM model used by Maven. It must match the value in the opening project tag. This example uses version 4.0.0 of the POM model.

- Lines 6-8: The groupId element defines the unique identifier of the project's group. This example uses the MicroProfile group.

- Lines 9-10: The artifactId element defines the unique identifier of the project itself. This example uses a Maven artifact called bookstore.

- Lines 11-12: The version element defines the version of the project. This example uses a SNAPSHOT version.

- Lines 13-14: The packaging element defines the type of artifact that will be generated by Maven. This example uses a WAR file.

- Lines 15-18: The properties element defines properties that can be used throughout the POM. This example defines the source and target Java versions for the Maven compiler plugin.

- Lines 19-20: The dependencies element defines the project's dependencies. This example depends on Jakarta EE 9.1 APIs and MicroProfile 5.0 APIs.

- Lines 21-34: The build element defines the project's build configuration. This example configures the Maven war plugin and the Liberty Maven plugin.

- Line 35: The finalName element defines the name of the generated artifact. This example uses a final name of bookstore.

- Lines 36-39: The pluginManagement element defines the project's plugin management configuration. This example configures the Maven war plugin and the Liberty Maven plugin.

- Lines 40-43: The plugins element defines the project's plugins. This example uses the Liberty Maven plugin.

Running an Existing Jakarta EE Project in Open Liberty

If you already have an existing application with Maven, just add the following Maven dependency to the pom.xml file:

```
<dependency>
    <groupId>io.openliberty</groupId>
    <artifactId>openliberty-runtime</artifactId>
    <version>[22.0.0.8,)</version>
    <type>zip</type>
</dependency>
```

This code will add the latest version of Open Liberty Runtime as a dependency to your project. During the build, it will download and install the Open Liberty Runtime ZIP file in the local Maven repository. The version field contains a range that will automatically select the latest version of Open Liberty Runtime that is compatible with your project. When you run the Maven build, it ensures that you are using the latest version of Open Liberty, but at least 22.0.0.8. If you want to use a specific version of Open Liberty, you can specify the version number in the version element.

When you build the project, Maven will generate a WAR file called product-ws. war in the target directory. When you're ready to move beyond the starter, continue developing your application by adding more dependencies to the POM file.

The server.xml Configuration File

A server.xml configuration file is provided with the necessary features for the MicroProfile and Jakarta EE versions that you previously selected.

```
<?xml version="1.0" encoding="UTF-8"?>
<server description="new server">

    <!-- Enable features -->
    <featureManager>
        <feature>jakartaee-9.1</feature>
        <feature>microProfile-5.0</feature>
    </featureManager>

    ...
    ...
```

```
<httpEndpoint id="defaultHttpEndpoint"
               httpPort="9080"
               httpsPort="9443" />

<!-- Automatically expand WAR files and EAR files -->
<applicationManager autoExpand="true"/>

<!-- Configures the application on a specified context root -->
<webApplication contextRoot="/api" location="product-ws.war" />

<!-- Default SSL configuration enables trust for default certificates
from the Java runtime -->
<ssl id="defaultSSLConfig" trustDefaultCerts="true" />
</server>
```

Explanation:

The server element is the root element of the server.xml file. The description element is a human-readable description of the server, which is set to new server in this case.

The featureManager element enables Jakarta EE 9.1 and MicroProfile 5.0 features. The httpEndpoint element defines the HTTP endpoint for the server. In this example, you use port 9080 for HTTP and 9443 for HTTPS.

The applicationManager element enables applications to be automatically expanded in the server. The webApplication element defines a web application in the server. This example uses the product-ws.war file and accesses it on the /product context root. The ssl element defines SSL configuration for the server. This example trusts default certificates from the Java runtime.

Developing a REST Application

A simple RestApplication.java file is generated for you to start creating your REST-based application.

```
package org.microprofile.rest;

import jakarta.ws.rs.ApplicationPath;
import jakarta.ws.rs.core.Application;

@ApplicationPath("/api")
```

```
public class RestApplication extends Application {

}
```

The jakarta.ws.rs.ApplicationPath annotation is used to specify the context root of the application. In this case, it is "/api". The RestApplication class is extending the jakarta.ws.rs.core.Application class to create a Jakarta RESTful web service application.

When you request this web service, you must include the contextRoot in the URL. For example, if you request the product resource, you need to make a request to http://localhost:9080/api/product.

Next, run the following command from the command line or terminal to start the Liberty server in development mode.

```
mvn liberty:dev
```

Using Open Liberty Plugin for IntelliJ IDEA Ultimate Edition

The Open Liberty plugin for IntelliJ IDEA Ultimate Edition is a plugin that provides support for developing applications on the Open Liberty server. If you want to work with Eclipse IDE, see Appendix C for further details.

Installing the Open Liberty Plugin in IntelliJ IDEA Ultimate Edition

This plugin is available from the JetBrains marketplace. You can install it from IntelliJ IDEA by choosing File ➤ Preferences ➤ Plugins and searching for "Open Liberty". Once you find the plugin, click Install and restart IntelliJ IDEA when prompted.

Once you install it, you'll see a Liberty option on the right in Figure 4-10. Clicking it, you'll see various Maven commands that you can run on your project. You can also start the Open Liberty server in Dev mode. See Figure 4-11.

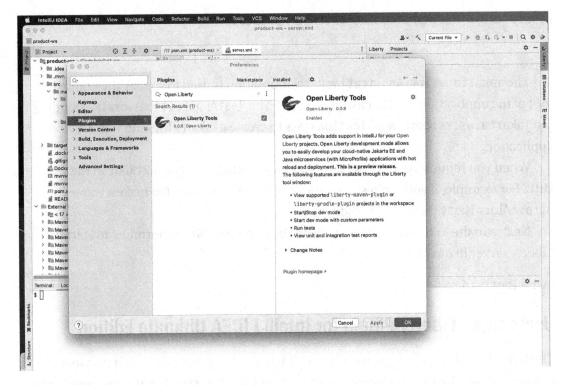

Figure 4-10. *Open Liberty Tools plugin*

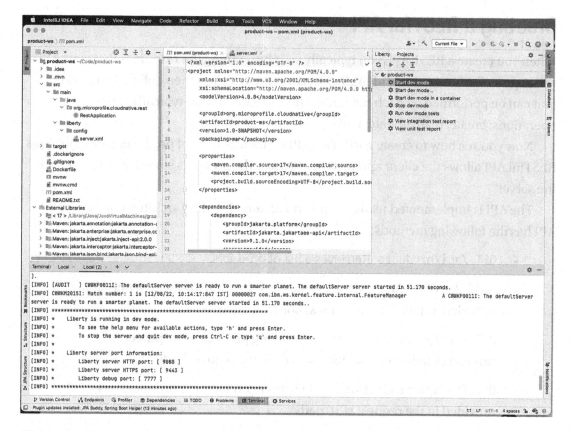

Figure 4-11. *Running Open Liberty server in dev mode using IntelliJ IDEA Ultimate Edition - Open Liberty Tools plugin*

This will start the Open Liberty server in development mode. If you make any changes to the source code, the server will automatically pick up the changes and redeploy the application. Also, if you make any configuration changes, like changing the HTTP port, the server will automatically pick up the changes.

Now change the contextRoot property in the server.xml file to /. The contextRoot element tells the server which directory to use as the root of the application. The original value was product-ws, meaning the server will look for files in the /wlp/product-ws directory. By changing it to /, you are telling the server to look for files in the /wlp/ directory.

Creating a RESTful API

When you create a REST API, you typically start by defining the resources that your API will expose. Each resource is identified by a unique URI. You then define the operations that can be performed on each resource. These operations are typically CRUD operations: create, read, update, and delete.

Now you see how to create a RESTful API to manage a list of products for a store. This RESTful API allows the client application to access the products stored as resources on the server.

The API is implemented using the Jakarta EE and the REST architectural style. The API has the following methods:

- `GET /api/products`: Retrieves a list of products.

- `POST /api/products`: Creates a new product; the product details are provided as JSON in the request body.

- `PUT /api/products`: Updates an existing product; the updated product details are provided as JSON in the request body.

- `DELETE /api/products/{id}`: Deletes a product; the product ID is provided in the request URL path.

Creating a Resource Class

A Resource class is an object that represents a specific REST resource, in this case a product. It contains the product's details, such as ID, name, price, quantity, and so on. For simplicity, this example only stores the ID and name. To implement a resource class first, you need to create a `Product` class, as shown:

```
public class Product {

    private Integer id;
    private String name;

    // default constructor
    public Product() {

    }
```

```java
// parameterized constructor     public Product(Integer id,
                                 String name) {

        this.id = id;
        this.name = name;
    }

// getters and setters
public Integer getId() {
        return id;
    }

public void setId(Integer id) {
    this.id = id;
}

public String getName() {
        return name;
    }

public void setName(String name) {
    this.name = name;
}

}
```

The Product class is a Plain Old Java Object. It has the id and name properties. You should declare a default constructor, getters, and setters for all fields. By doing this, you enable the Jackson library to convert your Java objects to JSON and vice versa. All properties must of Object type as well. Jackson cannot work with primitive types because they cannot be null. The id property is of type Integer, and name property is of type String. There are also getters and setters for the id and name instance variables. The getName() and getId() methods return the value of the respective property. The class also has two constructors. The first constructor is the default constructor. The second constructor takes in an id and name parameter and sets the values of the id and name properties to those values.

Creating a Service Class

A service class represents a collection of related resources. It includes methods for creating, updating, deleting, and retrieving (CRUD) operations on the resources.

You now create a ProductService class with a getProducts() method to return a list of Product objects:

```
package org.microprofile.cloudnative.rest;

import java.io.Serializable;
import java.util.*;

import jakarta.enterprise.context.ApplicationScoped;
import jakarta.ws.rs.*;
import jakarta.ws.rs.core.MediaType;
import jakarta.ws.rs.core.Response;

@Path("/products")
@ApplicationScoped
public class ProductService {

    private List<Product> products;

    public ProductService(){
        products = new ArrayList<>();

        products.add(new Product(Integer.parseInt("1"), "product 1"));
        products.add(new Product(Integer.parseInt("2") , "product 2"));
    }

    @GET
    @Produces(MediaType.APPLICATION_JSON)
    public List<Product> getProducts() {
        // Return a list of products
        return products;
    }
}
```

RESTful web services can produce and consume many different media types, including JSON, XML, and HTML. Annotations specify the media type that a method can consume or produce. For example, if a method is annotated with the following:

- @Consumes(MediaType.APPLICATION_JSON), it can consume JSON. Similarly, if a method is annotated with
- @Produces(MediaType.APPLICATION_XML), it can produce XML.

Both annotations are used together in a single method to support multiple media types. For example, - @Consumes(MediaType.APPLICATION_JSON) and - @Produces(MediaType.APPLICATION_XML) are used together in a single method, so the method can consume JSON and produce XML.

Table 4-2 shows a list of some of the popular media types, along with their constant fields in the jakarta.ws.rs.core.MediaType class and the corresponding HTTP ContentType.

Table 4-2. Popular Media Types and Their Constant Fields

Media Type	Constant Field in MediaType Class	HTTP ContentType
JSON	MediaType.APPLICATION_JSON	application/json
XML	MediaType.APPLICATION_XML	application/xml
HTML	MediaType.TEXT_HTML	text/html

The ProductService class is annotated with @ApplicationScoped. This will ensure that this class is available as long as the application is running. The ProductService class has a getProducts() method, which returns a list of products. This method is annotated with the @GET annotation, which maps this method to the GET HTTP method. The @Produces annotation tells the server that this method produces JSON content. This will return the following JSON response when you make a GET request to the /api/products endpoint.

To call this RESTful web service, you can type the https://localhost:9080/api/products URL in your browser. As shown in Figure 4-12, the response is an array of JSON objects. Each object has an id and name property. Note that only GET methods can be tested with browsers.

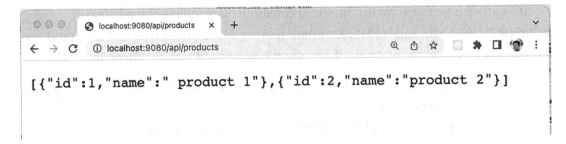

Figure 4-12. *The output of the RESTful web services in the browser*

To call all the HTTP methods (including PUT, POST, and DELETE), you can use a REST client such as Postman (www.postman.com/). See Figure 4-13.

Figure 4-13. *Calling RESTful web services using the Postman client*

Additionally, you can use the curl command-line utility to execute all the HTTP methods for your REST API. See Figure 4-14.

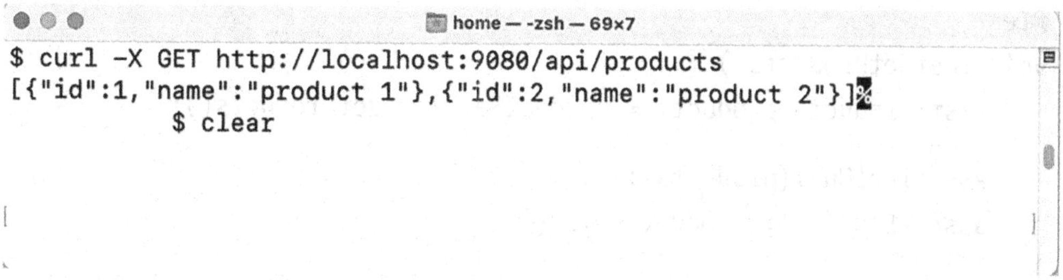

```
● ● ●                    🖥 home — -zsh — 69x7
$ curl -X GET http://localhost:9080/api/products
[{"id":1,"name":"product 1"},{"id":2,"name":"product 2"}]
                $ clear
```

Figure 4-14. *Calling RESTful web services using the curl command-line utility*

Writing Unit Tests for the Service Class

Unit tests can be written to test the service classes of a REST API. The following code demonstrates how to write a unit test using JUnit5 for the ProductService class:

```java
package org.microprofile.cloudnative.rest;
import org.junit.jupiter.api.AfterEach;
import org.junit.jupiter.api.BeforeEach;
import org.junit.jupiter.api.Test;

import java.util.List;

import static org.junit.jupiter.api.Assertions.assertEquals;
import static org.junit.jupiter.api.Assertions.assertNotNull;

class ProductServiceTest {

    private ProductService productService;

    @BeforeEach
    void setUp() {
        productService = new ProductService();
    }

    @AfterEach
    void tearDown() {
        productService = null;
    }
```

```
@Test
void testGetProducts() {
    List<Product> products = productService.getProducts();

    assertNotNull(products);
    assertEquals(2, products.size());
}
}
```

The testGetProducts() method tests the getProducts() method of the
ProductService class. The assertNotNull() and assertEquals() methods are used to
verify that the products list is not null and that it contains two products.

You can also execute the unit tests using your IDE. For example, in IntelliJ, you can
right-click the test class and select Run ProductServiceTest. In Eclipse, you can right-
click the ProductServiceTest class and select Run As ➤ JUnit Test. See Figure 4-15.

Figure 4-15. *Unit test execution using IntelliJ IDEA Ultimate Edition*

Updating Product Data Using REST APIs

After having successfully performed the development and testing of a GET method of ProductService to fetch the list of products resources, you'll now see how to create, update, and delete a product using the product's REST API. For this, you only need to add methods to the ProductService class.

Creating a Product

```
@POST
@Consumes(MediaType.APPLICATION_JSON)
public Response createProduct(Product product) {
    System.out.println("Creating product");
    products.add(product);
    return Response.status(Response.Status.CREATED)
            .entity("New product created").build();
}
```

Explanation:

The @POST annotation defines that the createProduct() method can be invoked via an HTTP POST request. The @Consumes annotation specifies that it will consume JSON data. This method takes a single parameter, which is of type Product. This parameter will be populated with the data sent in the HTTP POST request. The method creates a new Product object and adds it to the list of products. Finally, the method returns a Response object with a status code of 201 (Created) and a message indicating that a new product has been created. The output of the POST to the /api/products REST endpoint is shown in Figure 4-16.

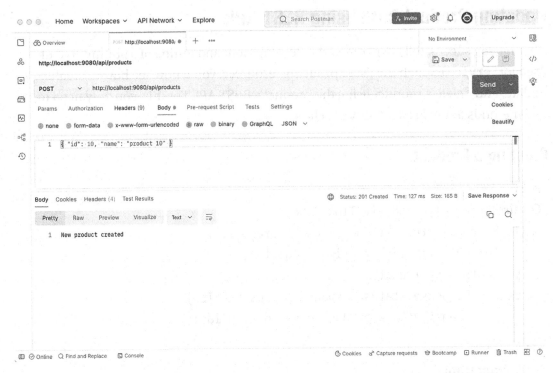

Figure 4-16. *The output of a POST request on the REST endpoint /api/products*

Updating a Product

```
@PUT
@Consumes(MediaType.APPLICATION_JSON)
public Response updateProduct(Product product) {
    // Update an existing product
    Response response;
    System.out.println("Updating product");
    for (Product p : products) {
        if (product.getId().equals(p.getId())) {
            p.setName(product.getName());
            response = Response.status(Response.Status.NO_CONTENT)
                    .entity("An existing product updated").build();
            return response;
        }
    }
    return Response.status(Response.Status.NOT_FOUND)
```

```
        .entity("Product with id->" + product.getId() + " does
        not exist")
        .build();
}
```

Explanation:

The @PUT annotation defines that the updateProduct() method can be invoked via an HTTP PUT request. The @Consumes annotation specifies that the method will consume JSON data. This method takes a single parameter, which is of type Product. This parameter will be populated with the data sent in the HTTP PUT request. The method iterates over the list of products and updates the product with the same id as the one sent in the request. If a product with the same id is not found, the method returns a 404 (Not Found) error. Finally, the method returns a Response object with a status code of 204 (No Content) and a message indicating that an existing product has been updated. The output of the POST to the /api/products endpoint is shown in Figure 4-17.

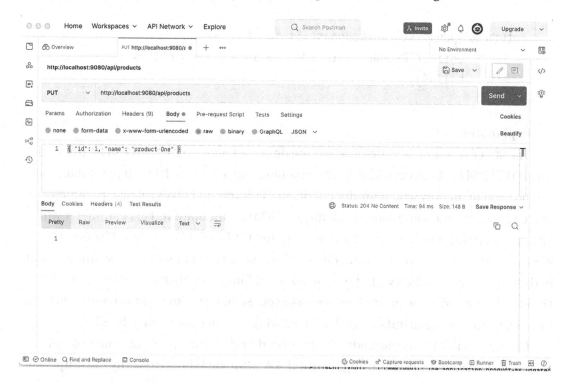

Figure 4-17. *The output of a PUT request on the REST endpoint /api/products*

Deleting a Product

```
@DELETE
@Path("products/{id}")
public Response deleteProduct(@PathParam("id") Integer id) {
    // Delete a product
    Response response;
    System.out.println("Deleting product with id: " + id);
    for (int i=0; i < products.size(); i++) {
        if (id.equals(products.get(i).getId())) {
            products.remove(i);
            response = Response.status(Response.Status.NO_CONTENT)
                    .entity("A product deleted").build();
            return response;
        }
    }
    return Response.status(Response.Status.NOT_FOUND)
            .entity("Product with id->" + id + " does not exist")
            .build();
}
```

Explanation:

The @DELETE annotation defines that the deleteProduct() method can be invoked via an HTTP DELETE request. The @Path annotation specifies the ID path parameter that will be used to identify which product to delete. This method takes a single parameter of type Integer and is annotated with the @PathParam annotation. This parameter will be populated with the id path parameter from the HTTP DELETE request. The method iterates over the list of products and deletes the product with the same id as the one sent in the request. If a product with the same ID is not found, the method returns a 404 (Not Found) error. Finally, the method returns a Response object with a status code of 204 (No Content) and a message indicating that an existing product has been deleted.

In addition to various methods discussed earlier in this chapter, you can also call the REST web services endpoints using IntelliJ IDEA Ultimate Edition to verify the output. Figure 4-18 shows the output of the DELETE request to the /api/products/{id} endpoint using the Endpoints tab of the IntelliJ IDEA Ultimate Edition IDE. This way developers do not need to switch to a different tool to preform development testing on their REST APIs under development.

Figure 4-18. *The output of a DELETE request on the REST endpoint /api/ products*

The code demonstrated in this chapter is not production quality; it was highly simplified in order to explain the fundamental principles of the REST API. In the upcoming chapters, you will learn how to build on this code. By implementing many features from the latest MicroProfile and Jakarta EE standards, you can make it a more robust microservice that is also cloud-ready. You also learn how to containerize, scale, deploy, and manage this application.

Summary

This chapter looked at how to create RESTful web services using the Jakarta EE RESTful web services APIs and how to deploy them to the Open Liberty application server. The chapter provided you with an overview of REST (Representational State Transfer). It then discussed the key features of the Open Liberty runtime. You learned about downloading and installing the Open Liberty application server. Finally, you were provided with the step-by-step instructions for running Jakarta EE applications in the Open Liberty application server. After reading this chapter, you should understand the basics of REST and should be able to create and deploy a RESTful web service using Open Liberty runtime on your own.

You also learned how to configure the Open Liberty server and develop RESTful APIs using the Open Liberty plugin for IntelliJ IDEA Ultimate Edition. Finally, you saw how to create and run unit tests for RESTful web services.

Some key takeaways from this chapter include:

- REST is an architectural style for building web services. REST has become the standard for designing web services, especially in the microservices world.

- Open Liberty is a flexible and lightweight runtime. You quickly develop, deploy, and execute RESTful web services on this platform.

- Open Liberty also provides complete support for the latest technologies and standards, such as MicroProfile and Jakarta RESTful Web Services. It also provides tools for quickly developing and testing applications like the Maven Liberty build plugin.

- You can use the Open Liberty plugin for IntelliJ IDEA Ultimate Edition for a better developer experience while developing REST applications. This plugin supports creating, running, and debugging Open Liberty applications from within the IDE.

This chapter covered RESTful web services at their very basic. The focus was to get you started with the process of building, testing, and deploying RESTful web services. Now you should be ready to introduce your own distinctive features of Jakarta EE Restful web services.

The next chapter dives deeper into the REST architectural pattern. You learn more about standard conventions, design considerations, best practices, and many advanced concepts related to building RESTful web services for cloud-native and microservices-based applications.

CHAPTER 5

Microservices Architecture

Service-based architecture has become an increasingly popular way to build scalable and resilient systems. It makes it possible to scale individual services independently by decoupling services from each other. It allows for more efficient use of resources and reduces the impact of failures on the overall system.

A service-based architecture is conceptually similar to an n-tier architecture, in which the functionality is divided into tiers, or layers. In a three-tier architecture, for example, the presentation layer (the interface to the user) is on one tier, the application logic layer (the code that implements the business logic) is on another tier, and the database layer (where the data is stored) is on the third tier. Each tier is responsible for a specific set of tasks, and the tiers are connected to each other through a network. This allows companies to scale their systems horizontally by adding more servers to a specific tier. This also makes it easier to manage system dependencies and updates.

Vertical Scaling

Vertical scaling is the process of increasing the capacity of a system by adding resources to the same level of hierarchy. It is also known as scaling up and involves adding more resources to a single server. The most common way to vertically scale an application is to simply add more RAM or CPU cores to the existing server(s). To perform vertical scaling, you first need to identify the resources that need to be increased. This may include RAM, CPU cores, or storage capacity. Once you know what needs to be upgraded, you can purchase new hardware or add more cores to your existing server.

© Tarun Telang 2023

T. Telang, *Beginning Cloud Native Development with MicroProfile, Jakarta EE, and Kubernetes*, https://doi.org/10.1007/978-1-4842-8832-0_5

The main advantage of vertical scaling is that it's usually the easiest and cheapest option to implement. In many cases, you can simply add more RAM or CPU cores to an existing server without having to purchase new hardware. Additionally, vertical scaling can be used to quickly respond to increases in demand. For example, if your website suddenly receives a surge of traffic, you can quickly add more resources to the server to handle the increased load.

While vertical scaling is usually the first step taken when increasing capacity, it does have its limitations. The main issue with vertical scaling is that at some point, you will reach the maximum capacity of the physical server, and adding more RAM or CPU cores to the existing server is no longer feasible. At this point, you'll need to either purchase new hardware or switch to horizontal scaling. It can be difficult to predict how much additional capacity you'll need in the future.

Vertical scaling can lead to "islands of capacity." For example, if you add a second server to your system, that server will likely have its RAM, CPU cores, and storage capacity. As a result, you'll now have two servers with different capacity levels. This can make it difficult to evenly distribute traffic across your system and may lead to one server being overloaded while the other has plenty of capacity.

Horizontal Scaling

Horizontal scaling is the process of adding more servers to a system. It's also known as scaling out. This can be done by adding new physical servers, or by using server virtualization to create multiple "virtual" servers on a single physical machine. In either case, the overall system capacity is increased by adding more servers.

The advantage of horizontal scaling is that it's often more scalable than vertical scaling. Since each new server starts with a clean slate, it can be fully utilized and doesn't need to be configured to work with the rest of the system. Additionally, horizontal scaling can be more efficient since each new server is typically used to its full capacity.

The disadvantages of horizontal scaling include increased complexity and higher costs. When you add more servers to a system, you need to keep track of all the different configurations and ensure that each server has the correct resources. This can be difficult to manage, especially if you're not using a configuration management system. Additionally, horizontal scaling often requires more hardware since each new server needs its own set of resources. As a result, horizontal scaling can be more expensive than vertical scaling.

Vertical vs. Horizontal Scaling

Which approach is best for your application depends on several factors, including cost, performance, scalability, and manageability. When deciding whether to use vertical or horizontal scaling, there are a few factors you should consider. First, think about how your system will grow in the future. If you anticipate a lot of growth, horizontal scaling may be a better option. Second, consider the costs associated with each approach. In general, vertical scaling is usually the easiest and cheapest option to implement, while horizontal scaling is more complex and expensive. However, horizontal scaling is often more scalable and easier to manage in the long run.

Vertical scaling can be less efficient than horizontal scaling. When you add more resources to a single server, those resources are often under-utilized. For example, if you add an additional CPU core to a server that's already running at 50 percent capacity, that new core will likely spend most of its time idle. In contrast, when you scale horizontally, each new server can be fully utilized since it's starting with a clean slate.

Finally, think about the complexity of your system. If you're not using configuration management, horizontal scaling can be more difficult to manage.

If you're not sure which approach is right for you, consider starting with vertical scaling and then switching to horizontal scaling if necessary. This will allow you to get started quickly and then scale up as needed. No matter which approach you choose, scaling is an important part of any system. By understanding the pros and cons of each approach, you can make sure that your system can handle the demands of growth.

History of Service-Based Architecture

The history of service-based architectures can be traced back to the early days of computing when organizations first started using computers to automate their business processes. Service-based architectures were originally designed to provide a way for different organizations to share information and resources without having to rely on a single, centralized computer system. In the early days of service-based architectures, organizations used a variety of methods to share information and resources, including point-to-point connections, client/server models, and distributed computing.

The concept of the service-based architecture grew out of earlier computing models such as client-server and n-tier architecture. In a traditional *client-server architecture*, a client makes requests to a server, which processes the requests and sends back the

113

response. Client-server architectures were typically used when processing requests require heavy computing needs that cannot be handled by client machines alone. It was the most popular style of computing in the 1980s and early 1990s. This model is centralized and inflexible because the server program had to be specifically designed to handle each different type of request.

In contrast, a service-based architecture is based on the idea of loose coupling, which means that services can be independent and can communicate with each other without requiring prior knowledge or planning. It makes it possible to build composite applications from existing services and to change or add services without affecting the rest of the application.

The use of web services has been a key enabler of service-based architectures. Web services are self-contained, modular applications that can be published, discovered, and invoked over the Internet. They use open standards such as XML and SOAP to promote interoperability.

The first generation of service-based architectures was characterized by a lack of standardization and interoperability. Each organization used its proprietary software and hardware, which made it difficult for different organizations to communicate and share information. These solutions emerged in the late 1990s led by companies such as BEA Systems, IBM, Microsoft, and Sun Microsystems. In addition, the early service-based architectures were not designed to support the Internet, which was not yet widely available.

The second generation of service-based architectures emerged in the late 1990s with the advent of the Internet and the need for organizations to be able to share information and resources across the globe. This new generation of service-based architectures was based on the principles of interoperability and standardization. The most notable example of a second-generation service-based architecture is the web services architecture, which was designed to allow different organizations to share information and resources using the Internet. The second generation of service-based architecture solutions was led by companies such as Oracle, SAP, and TIBCO.

The third generation of service-based architectures is currently emerging with the advent of cloud computing. Cloud computing is a new type of computing that allows organizations to use the Internet to access remote servers that are owned and operated by third-party providers. This new generation of service-based architectures is characterized by its ability to scale elastically and its pay-as-you-go pricing model. The most notable examples of a third-generation service-based architecture are the Amazon Web Services platform, the Google Cloud Platform, and Azure. The third generation of service-based architecture solutions is being led by companies such as Amazon, Google, and Netflix.

The fourth generation of service-based architectures is currently being developed and will likely be based on the principles of artificial intelligence (AI) and machine learning (ML). This new generation of service-based architectures will be able to learn and evolve to provide better services to users. The most notable example of a fourth-generation service-based architecture is the IBM Watson platform.

To summarize it all, service-based architectures have evolved to meet the changing needs of organizations. The first generation of service-based architectures was designed for a world without the Internet. The second generation was designed for a world with the Internet. The third generation is being designed for a world with cloud computing. And the fourth generation is being developed for a world with artificial intelligence and machine learning.

Types of Service-Based Architectures

The microservices and SOA architectures are the two popular types of service-based architectures.

Service-Oriented Architecture (SOA)

A *service-oriented architecture (SOA)* is an architectural style that enables the construction of loosely coupled, interoperable services. Services in an SOA can be discovered and invoked dynamically, and they can be composed into complex workflows. The term service-oriented architecture became popular in the early 2000s, when some companies, including SAP, IBM, and Microsoft, began to promote SOA as a way to build software systems. SOA is an evolution of the traditional monolithic application architecture, in which all components are tightly coupled and difficult to reuse. This architectural approach enables services to be loosely coupled, allowing them to be reused and composed to create new services.

SOA architectures are based on the idea of service-oriented computing, where services are self-contained units that can be accessed and used by other services. This type of architecture is advantageous because it promotes interoperability and the reuse of services. However, changing or adding new services to an existing SOA architecture can be more difficult.

SOA is not a specific technology or platform but rather a design approach that can be implemented using various technologies and platforms. SOA is often implemented using web services, which are self-contained, self-describing, modular applications that can be published, located, and invoked over the network. Web services use standards-based protocols such as HTTP to provide interoperability between different platforms and programming languages. These web services can be invoked by clients without the knowledge of the underlying implementation. This loose coupling of services also allows them to be quickly composed into new services or applications, providing greater flexibility and reusability.

What Is a Web Service?

A web service is a method of communication between two electronic devices over the World Wide Web. Although some web services can be accessed via a web browser, they are typically accessed through a software program that acts as a user interface, such as a web app or a website. Web services are often used to provide information or functionality to users, but they can also be used to communicate with other software programs. For example, a web service might allow a user to request directions from one location to another, or it might allow a user to send a text message to another user.

Web services are based on standards that allow different software programs to communicate. This allows developers to create new applications that can work with existing web services.

Some common standards for web services include:

- **SOAP (Simple Object Access Protocol)**: A standard that defines how two devices can exchange information over the Internet.

- **XML (Extensible Markup Language)**: A standard that defines how data can be structured and exchanged between devices.

- **WSDL (Web Services Description Language)**: A standard that defines how web services can be described and located on the Internet.

- **REST (Representational State Transfer)**: A standard that defines how web services can be accessed using the HTTP protocol.

- **JSON (JavaScript Object Notation)**: A standard that defines how data can be exchanged between devices in a format that is easy for humans to read and write.

What Is SOAP?

SOAP is short for Simple Object Access Protocol. It is an XML-based messaging protocol for exchanging information among computers. SOAP was designed to be independent of any particular programming model and other implementation details.

SOAP messages are composed of XML elements called *envelopes* that encapsulate the data being exchanged. The envelopes define the structure of the SOAP message and how it should be processed. A SOAP envelope can contain multiple headers and a body. The body contains the actual data being exchanged, while the headers can contain additional information about the message, such as the sender, recipient, and any processing instructions. Thus, SOAP offers a strong contract-based message format that can be used to access data from a variety of sources.

SOAP messages are typically transported over HTTP, but they can also be transported over other protocols. When transported over HTTP, SOAP messages are typically encoded using XML. While SOAP was designed to be independent of any particular transport protocol, HTTP is the most commonly used transport for SOAP messages.

SOAP is often used in combination with other web service technologies, such as WSDL and UDDI. WSDL is a standard for describing the functionality of a web service, while UDDI is a standard for listing available web services. Together, these technologies can be used to create a complete web service solution.

SOAP is a very powerful tool for building web services and can be used to access data from a variety of sources. However, because SOAP is based on XML, it can be quite verbose and require a lot of processing power to parse and generate SOAP messages. As a result, some developers prefer to use alternative technologies such as JSON or gRPC because they are more lightweight and require less processing power.

The original SOAP specification did not address security concerns. Therefore, the WS-Security specification was developed to extend SOAP with security features. WS-Security is now the most commonly used security standard for SOAP messages. Other specifications that extend to SOAP include WS-Addressing, which defines a standard way to include information such as the sender and recipient in a SOAP message, and WS-ReliableMessaging, which adds reliability features such as message delivery guarantees.

SOAP has been criticized for many reasons, including its complexity and the difficulty of debugging SOAP applications. However, it became popular, particularly in enterprise environments.

This next section discusses REST, which is an alternative to SOAP.

117

What Is REST?

REST stands for Representational State Transfer. It is an architectural style that defines a set of constraints and properties based on how web components communicate.

REST is often used in the context of web services, where it defines how resources are exposed and accessed by clients. A client can be any type of application that makes requests to a web service, such as a web browser, mobile app, or desktop application. In REST, the client is responsible for managing its own state, and the server is responsible for processing requests and returning responses. This separation of concerns simplifies application development and deployment.

REST defines a set of principles that are designed to make web services more scalable, flexible, and maintainable. These principles include:

- Resources are exposed as URI (uniform resource identifier) paths. A RESTful application should have a uniform interface that is consistent across all resources and operations. This makes the application easier to use and understand.

- HTTP methods are used to access and manipulate resources.

- Resources are represented in a format that is understandable by both clients and servers (usually JSON or XML).

- There is stateless communication between the client and server.

REST is often compared to other architectural styles, such as SOAP. However, there are some key differences between the two.

REST vs. SOAP

As you learned in previous sections, REST and SOAP are two popular web service technologies. The main difference between REST and SOAP is that REST is a lighter-weight protocol that doesn't rely on as much infrastructure as SOAP. This makes it less resource intensive, and therefore generally faster and less expensive to implement. REST can be built entirely on an open-source stack. SOAP, on the other hand, requires expensive software and hardware for development as well as for production deployment. REST is more distributable than SOAP too, as it can be easily deployed on a variety of platforms.

Additionally, REST is simpler than SOAP. REST services are often easier to develop and test than SOAP services. REST is more scalable than SOAP, as it is stateless. RESTful applications can be more easily scaled. In addition, REST is more flexible than SOAP because RESTful applications can be more easily extended and customized.

SOAP, on the other hand, is a more robust and feature-rich protocol. It includes support for security and transaction handling, which makes it well suited for mission-critical applications. SOAP services are also generally more interoperable than REST services since they can be used with a variety of programming languages and platforms.

Having discussed the service-oriented architecture options, the next section delves into the evolution of microservices.

The Monolithic Architecture

A monolithic architecture is the traditional unified model of software development. In this model, a software application is composed of a single, large codebase. This type of application is typically difficult to maintain and scale, due to its lack of modularity. A monolithic application is usually built as a single, self-contained unit, which can make it hard to add new features or update existing ones. Monolithic applications are often difficult to test and deploy because they require all of their dependencies to be installed and configured correctly. This can make it hard to ensure that the application will work correctly in different environments.

Monolithic applications can be a good choice for small projects that are not expected to grow very much over time. They can also be a good choice for projects that need to be very tightly coupled. However, for most applications, a more modular approach is typically a better choice.

Scalability is usually a major issue with monolithic applications. Because the entire application is built as a single unit, it can be hard to add new features or scale existing ones. Monolithic applications are often difficult to decompose into smaller services that can be deployed independently.

If you're considering using a monolithic application, you should also be aware of the potential difficulties that come with this type of application.

- **Fragile codebase:** A large codebase is difficult to maintain and there is a greater risk of introducing bugs.

- **Difficult to test:** It can be hard to test a monolithic application because all of its dependencies must be installed and configured correctly.

119

- **Deployment challenges:** Monolithic applications can be difficult to deploy because they require all of their dependencies to be installed and configured correctly.

- **Scalability issues:** Monolithic applications can be difficult to scale because they are not modular. It can be hard to add new features or scale existing ones.

Evolution of the Microservices Architecture

The origins of the microservices architecture can be traced back to the early days of distributed computing, when systems were designed to break large tasks into smaller parts that could be processed independently. This approach advocated for building systems out of small, composable services.

In the early 2000s, service-oriented architectures (SOA) emerged as a popular way to build distributed systems. The technologies like Web Services Description Language (WSDL) and Simple Object Access Protocol (SOAP) allowed developers to define and exchange services over HTTP.

However, SOA had some limitations. Firstly, it wasn't easy to scale SOA systems horizontally because each service had its dedicated infrastructure. Secondly, SOA systems were often complex and fragile, and it was difficult to manage dependencies between services.

In the 2010s, the microservices architecture emerged as a lightweight alternative to SOA. These systems are composed of small, modular services that can be deployed and operated independently. This approach is in contrast to a *monolithic architecture,* where all the components of a system are bundled into a single, large executable file. The most notable example of a microservices architecture is the Twitter platform.

Monolithic architectures are popular because they are simple and easy to understand. However, they have several drawbacks, including scalability and maintainability problems. On the other hand, microservices are based on the principles of modularity and decentralization, and they emphasize simplicity and scalability. Thanks to advances in DevOps tools and practices, it has become easier than ever to deploy and manage microservices-based systems.

Microservices Architectures

Microservices architectures structure an application as a collection of loosely coupled services. In a microservices architecture, services are fine-grained, and the protocols are lightweight. The benefits of decomposing an application into different, more minor services include the ability to develop, deploy, and scale the application more easily and independently. Microservices are typically deployed and managed using DevOps tools and practices.

The benefits of microservices include increased flexibility, improved scalability, and reduced costs. It is also a key enabler of the DevOps movement, which focuses on improving the speed and quality of software development.

When we talk about microservices, we usually refer to a software architecture pattern in which an application is composed of a suite of small, independently deployable services. These services communicate with each other via well-defined APIs and are deployed and scaled individually.

Benefits of Microservices Architectures

Microservices architectures have many benefits over the traditional monolithic architecture. One of the benefits of this approach is that it enables each service to be developed, deployed, and scaled independently, which can lead to faster development cycles and more agile deployments. In addition, each service can be written in a different language, which allows you to choose the best language for each service.

Another benefit of microservices is that this architecture can provide a higher level of fault tolerance, because if one service goes down, the others can continue to operate.

Microservices also help improve modularity and maintainability, since each service is typically responsible for a single task or functionality. This makes it easier to understand and modify the code for a particular service, and also helps prevent changes in one service from impacting other services. When a service needs to be updated, you can simply update the code for that service and deploy it without affecting the rest of the application. This makes it much easier to make changes to your application without breaking other parts of the system.

Finally, microservices can make implementing continuous delivery and deployment (CD/CI) pipelines easier, since each service can be deployed independently. It can lead to faster and more reliable deployments and reduced risk when making changes to the codebase.

In summary, the benefits of microservices include increased flexibility, improved scalability, and reduced costs. It is also a key enabler of the DevOps movement, which is focused on improving the speed and quality of software development.

Drawbacks of Microservices Architectures

While there are many benefits to using a microservices architecture, there are also some challenges that need to be considered. One of the biggest challenges is managing the communication between services, which can become complex as the number of services grows. In addition, microservices can introduce operational overhead, since each service needs to be deployed and managed independently.

Despite these challenges, microservices have become a popular architectural style for many modern applications. When used correctly, they can provide a number of benefits that can help improve the development process and the overall quality of the software.

Design Considerations

If you are thinking about decomposing your monolithic application into microservices, there are a few things you need to keep in mind. First, you need to carefully design the interfaces between services. The granularity of services is an important design consideration for microservices. A service should be fine-grained and focused on a single responsibility. This will make it easier to develop, deploy, and scale the service. In addition, it will make it easier to understand the service and its dependencies. Second, you need to manage and monitor the dependencies between services. It is also important to consider the dependencies between services when designing a microservices architecture. Each service should be independent and have no dependencies on other services. This will make it easier to deploy and manage the services. Finally, you need to be prepared for the challenges that come with managing a distributed system. These challenges include managing communication between services, managing data consistency, and dealing with failure.

Using Microservices in Cloud-Native Applications

Microservices are a popular architectural approach for building cloud-native applications. There are a number of benefits that can be gained by using cloud-native technologies, including:

- **Improved time to market:** Microservices can be deployed independently and quickly, allowing for a faster time to market.

- **Greater flexibility and scalability:** Each microservice can be updated or scaled independently, providing greater flexibility and scalability. This can be a major advantage over traditional monolithic applications, which can be more difficult to scale.

- **Reduced operational costs:** Cloud-native applications can use elastic compute resources on demand, which can reduce operational costs.

- **Improved resilience or fault tolerance:** Microservices can be restarted independently if one fails, improving fault tolerance. This is in contrast to a monolithic application, where a single failure can bring down the entire application.

There are also a few challenges that need to be considered when using microservices, including:

- **Increased complexity:** The increased number of moving parts can make debugging and troubleshooting more difficult. There is also a need for additional tooling to manage and monitor a microservices-based application.

- **Service discovery:** In a microservices architecture, each service needs to be able to discover and communicate with other services. This can be a challenge, particularly in large and complex applications.

- **Data consistency:** Because each microservice is independent, there is the potential for data inconsistencies to occur. This needs to be carefully managed to avoid issues.

Use the following best practices to get started with using microservices in your cloud-native applications:

- **Define your application's architecture upfront:** This will help you determine which services need to be built and how they will interact.

- **Use a service registry:** A service registry can be used to store information about the available services and their location. This can be useful for service discovery.

- **Use containerization:** Containerization can help reduce the overhead of managing and deploying microservices.

- **Use a microservices framework:** There are several microservices frameworks available that can help simplify the process of building and deploying microservices.

- **Handle data consistency carefully:** Data consistency is an important consideration in any distributed system.

The future of the service-based architecture is likely to be driven by the continued adoption of microservices and the rise of serverless computing.

Cloud-Native Twelve-Factor Applications

The *twelve-factor methodology* is a set of guidelines for designing and developing cloud-friendly applications. Following these guidelines can help improve performance, scalability, and resilience. Applications that are designed and developed using the twelve-factor methodology are known as *cloud-native twelve-factor applications*.

1. **Codebase:** A twelve-factor app is always tracked in a version control system, such as Git, and deployed from there. This makes it easy to roll back changes if necessary and maintain a history of your codebase.

2. **Dependencies:** All dependencies, such as libraries and frameworks, should be declared in a manifest, such as a POM file for Maven-based Java projects so that they can be easily installed and updated.

3. **Config:** Configuration should be stored in the environment, rather than in the code, so that it can be easily changed without changing the code itself.

4. **Backing services:** Twelve-factor apps are designed to use external backing services, such as databases and message queues. They should be treated as attached resources. This means that they can be easily detached and replaced without affecting the running code.

5. **Build, release, run:** Twelve-factor applications are built using a repeatable and automatable process that includes tests to ensure quality. This ensures that they can be released at any time. They are then released as immutable artifacts that can be deployed easily and quickly. Finally, they are run in an isolated environment, such as a container, so that they can be scaled up or down as needed.

6. **Processes:** Twelve-factor applications are designed to be run as stateless processes. The application is divided into small, self-contained processes. Each process can be started, stopped, or restarted independently as needed without affecting the others.

7. **Port binding:** Twelve-factor applications are designed to be deployed on a server that exports a port for them to bind to. This makes it easy to run multiple instances of the app on the same server and also makes it easy to change the server if necessary.

8. **Concurrency:** Twelve-factor applications are designed to be run in a concurrent environment so that they can take advantage of modern computing resources, such as a cluster of servers. Different parts of the app can be run at the same time on different cores or machines. This also allows them to be scaled up or down as needed.

9. **Disposability:** Twelve-factor applications are designed to be started or stopped quickly. This makes it easy to deploy new versions or roll back changes if necessary without affecting the overall application.

10. **Dev/prod parity:** Twelve-factor applications are designed to have the same environment in development as in production. This makes it easier to catch errors early and avoid surprises when deploying to production.

11. **Logs:** Logging is the process of tracking the events that occur in a system. Logging can be used to improve the operations of a system and prevent problems from occurring in a system by tracking the events that are important to the system. Twelve-factor applications treat logs as event streams. This makes it easy to aggregate and process them for monitoring and analysis.

12. **Admin processes:** Twelve-factor applications have separate processes for administering the app, such as running database migrations. This separation of concerns makes it easier to manage the app and avoid errors.

What Is a Virtual Machine?

A *virtual machine* is a software program that imitates a physical computer. It allows one computer to run multiple operating systems and applications simultaneously.

Virtual machines have many benefits over physical machines. They are easier to deploy, manage, and scale. They also allow for greater flexibility and resource utilization. Additionally, virtual machines are not limited by hardware constraints and can be easily migrated to different hosts.

Virtual machines are useful for testing software and applications in different environments without affecting the host computer. They are also used to run multiple operating systems on a single computer.

One of the main disadvantages of virtual machines is that they can be less stable than physical machines. Additionally, virtual machines can be resource-intensive, requiring more CPU, memory, and storage than physical machines. They can also be more complex to manage and troubleshoot.

Virtual machines are made possible by virtualization software, which creates a virtual environment for the guest operating system to run in. Virtualization software provides a layer of abstraction between the guest operating system and the host hardware, making it possible to run multiple guests on one host.

A virtual machine is a computer that runs on another computer. The other computer is called the host, and the computer running on it is called the guest. Hardware infrastructure is the electronic and physical components that make up a computer system. This includes the central processing unit (CPU), memory, storage, input/output devices, and networking hardware.

Virtualization is the process of creating a virtual machine. This can be done using software that emulates hardware or by running a hypervisor on top of existing physical hardware. Virtualization software provides a layer of abstraction between the guest operating system and the host hardware, making it possible to run multiple guests on one host.

Hypervisors are a type of virtualization software that allows multiple guest operating systems to run on a single host. The most common type of hypervisor is a bare-metal hypervisor, which runs directly on the host's hardware. Other types of hypervisors include hosted and para-virtualized.

Bare-metal hypervisors are typically used in enterprise environments where performance and stability are critical. Hosted hypervisors are typically used in smaller environments or for testing and development purposes. Para-virtualization is a type of virtualization that requires special software to be installed on the guest operating system for it to run properly.

There are many benefits to using virtual machines, including the ability to run multiple operating systems on one computer, the ability to migrate guests from one host to another easily, and the ability to isolate guests from each other.

Virtual machines have some drawbacks, as well. They can be more resource-intensive than running a single operating system on a computer, and they can be less stable than natively running operating systems. Despite these drawbacks, virtual machines are popular due to the many benefits they offer.

What Are Containers?

Containers are a type of virtualization that allows you to isolate an application or service from the underlying operating system (OS). This enables you to run multiple containers simultaneously on a single OS instance.

Each container has its isolated environment in which it can run without affecting other containers or the host OS. This makes containers an ideal solution for microservices, which are small, self-contained services that can be deployed and scaled independently.

Containers are often compared to virtual machines (VMs). Both VMs and containers provide isolation and allow you to run multiple instances on a single host. However, there are some key differences between these two types of virtualization.

VMs are heavier and more resource-intensive than containers. They require a full OS instance to be running inside each VM, which can lead to inefficient use of resources.

In contrast, containers share a single OS kernel and only include the libraries and files they need to run, making them much lighter and more efficient. This enables you to run more containers on a single host than you could VMs.

Another key difference is that VMs are typically used to run entire applications, while containers are typically used for individual services or components of an application. This makes it easier to deploy and scale applications using containers.

If you're looking for a way to virtualize your applications and services, containers are a great solution. They're lightweight, efficient, and easy to deploy and scale.

What Are Container-Based Applications?

Containers are lightweight virtual machines or self-contained units of deployment. They allow you to package all the dependencies necessary to run your application in a self-contained unit. Running an application using containers means that you must first package your application and its dependencies to run in a container like Docker. Then you can run these containers on any server, as shown in Figure 5-1.

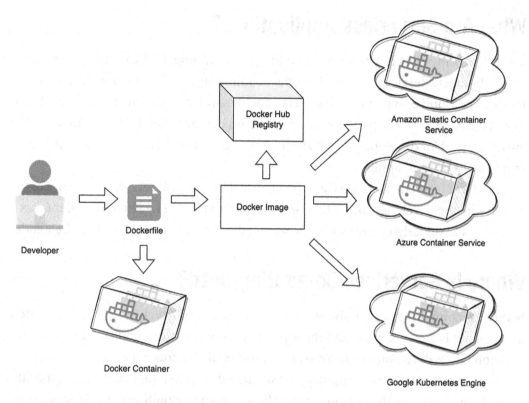

Figure 5-1. *Container-based applications*

To run an application in a container, start by building an image (such as a Docker image), which is a template used to create a container. You can create images using a text file known as a Dockerfile, which contains instructions describing how to build a Docker image. With unique configurations and settings, you can use this image to create as many containers as you want. You can then run them anywhere without requiring other libraries or tools, as long as you have a container runtime technology like Docker Engine installed.

Since containers offer an isolated environment for your code; they're ideal for deployments on cloud platforms like Amazon Web Services (AWS), Google Cloud Platform, and Microsoft Azure. You can also use a container orchestration platform like Kubernetes to deploy and manage containers at scale. This makes them suitable for deployments in the cloud, as you can quickly move them from one server to another without worrying about compatibility issues.

What Are Serverless Applications?

Serverless computing is a new way of building and running applications. It's also known as functions as a service, or FaaS. Serverless computing is a cloud-computing execution model. The cloud provider runs the server and dynamically allocates machine resources to run the code, scaling up or down depending on demand. Serverless computing takes away the need for developers to provision, manage, and operate servers, leaving them free to focus on their applications.

The term "serverless" is misleading because there are still servers involved. This just means that the developers don't have to worry about them. The cloud provider takes care of all the underlying infrastructure so that the developers can focus on their code.

Where Is Serverless Computing Used?

Serverless computing is a relatively new concept and is still evolving. It's not yet widely adopted but is growing in popularity, especially among startups and small businesses that don't have the resources to invest in a traditional IT infrastructure.

You can use serverless computing for small, independent tasks that your application needs to perform quickly and efficiently. These tasks are usually event-driven, such as handling a user upload or processing a payment.

You can also use serverless computing for larger and more complex applications by dividing the application into smaller components, with each element handled by a different serverless function.

Some of the most popular use cases for serverless computing are:

- **Web applications**—You can use serverless computing to host static websites and dynamic web applications.

- **Mobile applications**—You can also use serverless functions to power the backend of mobile applications. They can handle user authentication, database queries, push notifications, and other common tasks.

- **Internet of Things (IoT)**—You can use it to process data from sensors and devices in real time. You can also use it to trigger actions, such as sending a notification or activating a device.

- **Data processing**—You can use serverless functions to handle transactions and payments. You can also use it to send receipts and notifications.

- **Machine learning (ML)**—You can use serverless functions to train and deploy machine learning models.

Benefits of Serverless Computing

Serverless computing offers the following benefits over traditional computing models, such as virtual machines or containers:

- **Reduced costs**—There is no need to invest in, or maintain, servers. You only pay for the resources you use, and there are no upfront costs. There's no need to pay for idle capacity or unutilized servers. This can lead to significant cost savings, especially for applications with variable or unpredictable workloads.

- **Increased agility**—Serverless computing allows you to deploy code quickly, and it can automatically scale up or down to meet the demands of your users. You can even handle sudden spikes in traffic without any problems.

- **Improved focus**—By taking away the need to manage servers, serverless computing allows you to focus on developing and deploying your applications. You can focus on your code and let the serverless platform handle the rest. This can make your life easier as a developer.

Drawbacks of Serverless Computing

Despite its many benefits, serverless computing does have some drawbacks.

- **Difficult to debug and troubleshoot problems**—One of the main drawbacks of serverless computing is that it can be more challenging to debug and troubleshoot problems because you don't have direct access to the underlying servers.

- **Reduced flexibility**—Serverless computing can be less flexible than other hosting options because you're limited to the resources that the serverless platform provides.

- **Vendor lock-in**—It can lead to vendor lock-in, making it difficult to switch to a different platform if you're not happy with your current provider.

- **Lack of support**—Because it's still a new technology, there's a lack of support and documentation for serverless computing. It can be challenging to find answers to your questions or get help when you're stuck.

Popular Serverless Platforms

If you're looking for a new way to build and run your applications, you should check out serverless computing. It's a great way to save money on infrastructure costs and automatically scale your applications. Here are some of the most popular serverless platforms to explore:

- Amazon Web Services Lambda

- Azure Functions

- Google Cloud Functions

- IBM Cloud Functions

- Apache OpenWhisk

Each platform has its strengths and weaknesses, so you'll need to choose the right one for your project.

Main Components of a Serverless Computing Platform

Serverless platforms are usually built on top of cloud infrastructure platforms like Amazon Web Services (AWS), Microsoft Azure, or Google Cloud Platform (GCP). These platforms provide all the necessary resources to run your code, including storage, networking, and computing resources. The main components of a serverless computing platform are:

- **Functions**—These are the pieces of code that you write and deploy to the serverless platform. Each function can be triggered by an event, such as a user upload or a payment.

- **Events**—These are the events that trigger your functions—for example, a user upload or a payment.

- **Storage**—This is where your code and data are stored.

- **Networking**—This is how your functions communicate with each other and with the outside world.

- **Computing resources**—These are the resources that your functions need to run, such as CPU and memory.

Serverless applications run in a completely stateless environment. In a serverless application, you use a Function as a Service (FaaS) that packages and deploys code as a standalone executable. The code responds to events like an incoming HTTP request or a file upload to an S3 bucket. Running a serverless application means you don't need to provision or manage traditional servers. The cloud provider's infrastructure executes the application as required and shuts it down when it's no longer necessary. Several FaaS offerings include AWS Lambda, Azure Functions, and Google Cloud Functions. Serverless applications can significantly simplify deploying and managing applications, as there is no need to worry about servers or scaling. See Figure 5-2.

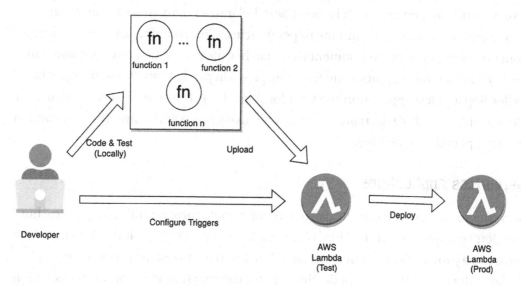

Figure 5-2. *Serverless application*

This approach is simpler to manage than using containers and can be cheaper since you only pay for the time your code is running. However, serverless deployments are less flexible and can be less efficient.

Serverless Applications vs. Containers

In the world of cloud-based computing, there are two main approaches to deploying applications: containers and serverless applications. Each has its advantages and disadvantages. So which one is right for your applications? Now that you have a basic understanding of these approaches, let's look at the pros and cons of each.

Ease of Development

Developers are constantly under pressure to quickly produce high-quality code. This can be a daunting task, especially when you're working with a new technology. Ease of development is the ability to develop an application quickly and easily. This can be measured in a number of ways, such as how quickly you can get up and running, how easy it is to make changes, and how many errors you encounter.

Container-Based Applications

You can develop containerized applications using a framework or programming language of your choice, which is then compiled into a binary that can run on any machine that has the same runtime dependencies. With containers, you can quickly spin up a development environment that matches the production environment. This allows for faster development and fewer surprises in production. It also makes it easy to develop and test applications on your local machine. If you're already familiar with Docker and know how to create images, you'll likely be up and running with a container-based application in no time.

Serverless Applications

Serverless applications typically use one of the popular programming languages, but you don't compile them into a binary. Instead, you package them into a function. You must use a provider's portal or command-line interface to test and deploy them. It's easier to develop serverless applications than their containerized counterparts. This is because you don't need to worry about setting up or managing containers or servers. The provider takes care of that for you. This allows you to focus on developing your code. You can also build and test your code in a local environment.

Ease of Deployment

Deployment is a critical process, as it places code into production. It includes configuring code for use in a live environment, testing it to ensure that it works as expected, and then deploying it to one or more servers. Once you deploy the code, you need to configure and manage your environment so that it runs smoothly and meets your business or organizational needs

Container-Based Applications

Container-based applications are easy to deploy, as you can package them and move them to any server without worrying about compatibility issues. You can also use a container orchestration platform like Kubernetes to deploy and manage containers at scale. Containerized applications can also be deployed using automation tools like Puppet, Chef, or Ansible. This makes it easy to deploy them on multiple machines.

Serverless Applications

With a serverless application, you don't need to provision any infrastructure, but you do need an FaaS provider. These providers offer a more limited set of features than container platforms. Serverless applications are deployed using a cloud provider's portal or command-line interface. This might require a learning curve, but it's usually easy. There is no guarantee that the deployment will always go smoothly. Each provider has different methods of deploying an application, and it's your responsibility to set up and maintain your code. While there are many public libraries and tools, it can be difficult to find the right one for your specific application and platform.

Cloud Computing Cost

Many companies depend on public cloud services providers for their infrastructure needs. Cloud computing cost is the cost for the use of cloud services like compute, storage, and networking resources.

Container-Based Applications

Container-based applications can be more expensive to run than serverless applications. This is because containers typically require more resources (e.g., CPU, memory, disk). As a result, your cloud bill will be higher if you choose to deploy a container-based application on a public cloud provider.

Serverless Applications

Serverless applications are often much cheaper to run than container-based applications. This is because you only pay for the time your application is actually executing rather than the entire time your servers are running (which can be 24/7). Additionally, serverless applications automatically scale to meet demand, so you don't have to worry about provisioning extra servers when your traffic spikes.

Portability

Portability is the ability to move an application from one provider to another with relative ease.

Container-Based Applications

You can move a container-based application from one provider to another with minimal effort. Cloud-native applications are built to take advantage of the cloud. They're designed to be portable, scalable, and resilient. In a cloud-native application, you'll typically find microservices that you can deploy and scale easily.

Container-based applications are a great fit for cloud-native applications. Containers make it easy to package and deploy code as a standalone executable. They also allow you to run multiple containers on the same server, making it easy to scale your application.

Serverless Applications

Serverless applications are not as portable as container-based applications. This is because a serverless application is tightly coupled with the provider's infrastructure. If you want to move your application to another provider, you will likely need to spend a significant amount of time and effort modifying your code. One of the main disadvantages of using serverless applications is vendor lock-in. Vendor lock-in occurs when you're locked into a specific vendor and can't easily switch. This can be a problem if the provider you're locked in to decides to raise prices or change the terms and conditions.

Scalability and Performance

Scalability measures how well a system or application can maintain performance as it supports an increased number of users or traffic. Performance is how quickly a system or application performs when handling a given level of workload.

Container-Based Applications

Containerized applications are typically much more scalable than serverless applications because you can easily add or remove containers to meet your scaling needs. Additionally, containers offer a higher degree of isolation than serverless applications. If one container fails, it will not impact others. However, this can be a problem with serverless applications.

Serverless Applications

A serverless platform maintains scalability and performance in response to incremental load challenges. It is not suitable for applications that require quick responses. You may experience some latency compared to running your application on dedicated servers because a cloud provider executes serverless applications on demand.

Security Considerations

Security is always a critical consideration for any application.

Serverless Applications

By default, serverless applications are secure. Serverless platform providers take care of many security tasks, such as patching, that you would otherwise have to do yourself. Additionally, most FaaS providers offer built-in security features, such as encryption and access control.

However, serverless applications can be vulnerable to dedicated denial-of-service (DDoS) attacks. Because your application is running on a provider's infrastructure, a hacker may be able to send many requests to your application at once, overwhelming it and taking it down.

You generally use popular frameworks like Node.js to create serverless applications, which might have some inherent security flaws. If your application is not adequately secured, hackers could compromise it.

Container-Based Applications

You can make container-based applications more secure than serverless applications. By running them on dedicated infrastructure, you can better safeguard your application than if you use a cloud provider's infrastructure.

Additionally, because containers are self-contained, it's usually more difficult for hackers to access the code and data. However, you need to manage the security of your containers yourself, which can be difficult if you're not a security expert.

If you need a high degree of isolation or scalability, containers may be the right choice. However, if you need simplicity and ease of development, serverless may be the way to go. Container-based applications offer more flexibility and control than serverless but require more management and expertise. But there are also some potential downsides to using containers. They require you to manage and configure servers, and they can be more challenging to develop than serverless applications.

Microservice Deployment Patterns

Microservices architectures are the most popular trend in application development. They are a great way to develop faster and deliver better solutions for your customers and users. Deploying microservices is critical for organizations. Microservices enable your development team to roll out software solutions more quickly and better react to customer needs.

This is possible because developers can also speed up their development and testing cycles, reduce errors, and fix bugs quickly. Although microservice architectures provide various benefits, they have some drawbacks due to the additional complexities involved.

Key Considerations

Here are some key considerations related to microservices deployment that any organization must understand:

- Having many services, dependencies, and interactions at runtime can make the project difficult to manage.

- Communication among multiple microservices brings more chances of failure. Your development teams must be very familiar with distributed systems. They must be able to address issues resulting from network latency and load balancing.

- Your development team also needs the right DevOps, networking, and security skills to deliver microservices. Your team also has to understand the concepts, coding style, and test cases, which might take more time and effort.

- Upgrades and rollout of microservices requires lots of coordination between various engineering teams. In addition, your team must perform complex testing over distributed environments. Fortunately, microservices deployment strategies can help you overcome these challenges and minimize downtime.

Microservices Deployment Strategies and Patterns

The microservices deployment pattern is a technique for updating and modifying software components. A microservices deployment pattern or strategy enables easy deployments and allows you to modify microservices.

The following subsections list the microservice deployment patterns that help improve microservices availability.

Canary Deployment

This is a well-known strategy in microservices deployment. A *canary* is a candidate version of microservices that get a small percentage of traffic.

This includes releasing the microservice with the new version to only a small percentage of load first and seeing if it works as expected. As the microservice passes through rigorous testing, it gradually encounters larger workloads. If canaries aren't functioning correctly, traffic may be routed to a stable version while the problem is investigated and debugged. Canary rollback is the process of rolling back microservices regularly.

The canary deployment strategy releases only one microservice at a time. Microservices with higher criticality and risks involved can be made available before others. It improves availability by detecting problems early, before a critical microservice is exposed to the entire system.

Pitfalls of Canary Deployment

The biggest potential pitfall with this approach is that it might release microservices too early. Canary releases are usually smaller microservices with limited traffic. Frequent issues during deployments can also slow down development.

Blue-Green Deployment

The blue-green deployment strategy involves maintaining two microservice variations simultaneously in production. One microservice version (the blue microservice) is visible to the user and gets traffic. The other one (the green microservice) remains idle for developers to make updates. A microservice remains in a blue state until it passes tests and is ready to go out. After passing all tests, microservices move to the green state, where they get traffic and are visible to users. However, microservices are constantly being monitored to detect if the microservice is performing well or needs to revert back to the blue state.

Blue-green deployment can improve availability by keeping the microservices available during development and deployment. There's no downtime during development and deployment because there's always another stable variation serving production traffic. In addition, if the new deployment isn't working correctly, you can quickly roll back to the previous variation (i.e., the blue microservice).

Pitfalls of the Blue-Green Deployment Strategy

The possibility of microservice version mismatch is a potential pitfall with blue-green deployment. Another pitfall is that microservices need constant monitoring to detect issues. This leads to increased costs and time.

Dark Launching

A dark launch is a technique that deploys updates to microservices catering to a small percentage of the user base. It does not affect the entire system. When you dark launch a new feature, you initially hide it from most end-users. The launch audience can vary depending on use case and business requirements. The process of dark launching involves building a new version of the microservices in an environment that's separate from the production environment.

Once the feature has been tested, you deploy it in a pre-production or test environment, and gradually increase the rollout until all users are exposed to it. Subsequently, if you see the feature performing well, you continue to deploy it to serve more users.

Feature toggles are a good way to release your updates gradually. You can easily turn the feature on or off. In this way, you can test its impact without having it be totally live. You can choose what traffic to route to the microservices that are behind feature toggles during the testing phase. When the microservice has been tested and found to be suitable under realistic loads, it is activated to serve traffic from the entire production environment.

One of the biggest benefits of dark launching is that you can perform more tests before releasing your product. This lets you catch bugs early, thus saving time and cost associated with fixing bugs in production.

Dark launching also allows your development team to test the new system architecture before end-users can see it. This strategy allows controlled deployments to pre-determined audiences who are statistically likely to use the microservice. This will enable you to gain vital insights before deployment to production.

Pitfalls of Dark Launching

The biggest potential pitfall with dark launching is that it may release microservices early. Another drawback is that microservices are behind feature toggles, which can lead to increased costs and time for debugging microservices. Additionally, to enable continuous development, teams must be able to move microservices behind feature toggles during development.

Staged Release

The staged release deployment strategy for microservices involves gradually releasing microservices to one environment at a time. For example, your development team should first release microservices to the testing environment and later to production.

Don't enable microservices in production until you know that they're safe in a testing environment. The staged release strategy incrementally deploys each service. This ensures longer time between failures for each service than if they were simultaneously deployed. It maintains high availability by staggering failures across multiple services over time. This also provides better recovery capabilities.

Pitfalls of Staged Release

In this approach, there may be downtime while microservices are introduced in new environments. Deploying huge batches of change might make it difficult for the development team to diagnose and recover from failures. In addition, your development must deploy all the changes in a single batch. This means any errors will require them to roll back the entire release process for each microservice.

Microservices Management

Deploying microservices can be very challenging to organizations with limited engineering know-how or without best practices in place. Technology choices also play a role since some microservices require more management, especially microservices that are in high-velocity platforms. These microservices require constant attention to improve their performance, security, scaling, and so on.

Summary

In this chapter, you learned about microservices architectures. You also saw various other popular approaches to software design and their pros and cons. When implemented correctly, microservices can help you create applications that are composed of loosely coupled services and that are easier to manage and scale. However, there are also some challenges associated with using this architectural style. It is important to have a strategy for handling failures between services and carefully consider how your services will interact. In the next chapters, you learn how to implement a complete microservices solution using Eclipse MicroProfile. You also learn about how to deploy them in Docker containers and orchestrate them using Kubernetes.

CHAPTER 6

The Eclipse MicroProfile Framework

In this chapter, you will be introduced to the Eclipse MicroProfile architecture. The chapter also covers the essential and most critical standards in the Eclipse MicroProfile, namely configuration, health checking, fault tolerance, metrics, RESTful web services, open tracing, and open API.

What Is the Eclipse MicroProfile Framework?

The Eclipse MicroProfile (`https://microprofile.io/`) is an standard that provides a modular set of Jakarta EE (`https://jakarta.ee/)` and microservices-related features that are suitable for application development in a microservices architecture. The goals are to optimize Enterprise Java for a microservices architecture, promote the use of common standards, and avoid vendor lock-in.

The Eclipse MicroProfile specification addresses the challenges of microservices, such as distributed tracing, health checking, and security. It also provides APIs for reactive programming, JSON processing, and RESTful web services.

The MicroProfile project (`https://projects.eclipse.org/projects/technology.microprofile)` was started in 2016 by Red Hat, IBM, Payara, Tomitribe, and LJC (London Java Community). The project is now run as an open-source project under the Eclipse Foundation. MicroProfile is a set of specifications providing a microservices framework. It defines several Jakarta EE specifications and APIs to make it easier to develop and deploy microservices.

© Tarun Telang 2023
T. Telang, *Beginning Cloud Native Development with MicroProfile, Jakarta EE, and Kubernetes*,
https://doi.org/10.1007/978-1-4842-8832-0_6

Layers of Functionality in MicroProfile

MicroProfile is designed to work with Jakarta EE. It has three layers of functionality. The bottom layer includes RESTful web services, REST clients, dependency injection, JSON processing, and reactive streams operators. The middle layer has features like Open API, config, fault tolerance, and security (JWT propagation). The top layer has features like metrics, tracing, and health checking. Figure 6-1 depicts these three layers.

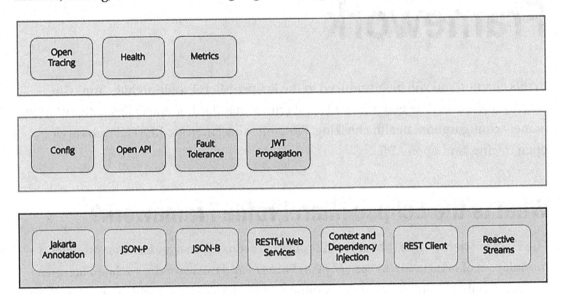

Figure 6-1. *Three layers of functionality in MicroProfile*

Open Liberty provides full support of all three layers of MicroProfile functionality. The following standards are present in the bottom layer:

- **Jakarta Annotations** (https://jakarta.ee/specifications/ annotations/): Open Liberty supports the latest version of Jakarta annotations, which is the de facto standard for annotations in Java. The Jakarta Annotations API enables you to write type-safe, declarative code.

- **JSON-P** (https://jakarta.ee/specifications/jsonp/): The JSON Processing (or JSON-P) APIs provide a portable way to parse and generate JSON data. Jakarta JSON Processing is part of the Jakarta EE specification and is included in Open Liberty.

- **JSON-B** (https://jakarta.ee/specifications/jsonb/): The JSON Binding (JSON-B) APIs provide a standard binding layer for converting Java objects to and from JSON documents. Open Liberty provides built-in support for Jakarta JSON Binding (JSON-B).

- **RESTful web services** (`https://jakarta.ee/specifications/restful-ws/`): This provides a standard way to write RESTful web services. RESTEasy is a portable implementation of this specification included in Open Liberty. You can create a REST API using this.

- **CDI** (`https://jakarta.ee/specifications/cdi/`): Contexts and Dependency Injection (CDI) enables you to manage the lifecycle of stateful components and inject dependencies into your components.

- **REST Client** (`https://microprofile.io/project/eclipse/microprofile-rest-client`): REST Client enables you to write type-safe, declarative code to invoke RESTful web services. It provides APIs specification for invoking REST services.

- **Reactive Streams** (`https://microprofile.io/project/eclipse/microprofile-reactive-streams`): The Reactive Streams specification provides a standard for asynchronous stream processing with non-blocking backpressure. It also provides API specifications for working with reactive streams. The *smallrye-reactive-streams* operators are a portable implementation of this specification included in Open Liberty.

The following specifications comprise the middle layer of MicroProfile specifications:

- **Config** (`https://microprofile.io/project/eclipse/microprofile-config`): The Config layer provides a uniform mechanism for accessing configuration data from multiple sources. It provides API specifications for injecting configuration properties into applications. This includes properties files, system properties, environment variables, and JSON documents.

- **Open API** (https://microprofile.io/project/eclipse/
  microprofile-open-api): The Open API specification enables you
  to write documentation for your RESTful web services in a standard
  format. This documentation can be used by tools such as Swagger UI
  to generate interactive documentation for your web services.

- **JWT Propagation** (https://microprofile.io/project/eclipse/
  microprofile-jwt-auth): The JWT Propagation specification
  enables you to propagate security tokens (such as JSON Web Tokens)
  across components in a microservices architecture. It provides APIs
  for authenticating using JSON Web Token.

- **Fault Tolerance** (https://microprofile.io/project/eclipse/
  microprofile-metrics): The Fault Tolerance layer provides APIs
  and annotations that can be used to write fault-tolerant code and
  handle failures in your cloud-native application gracefully. This
  includes APIs specification for timeouts, retries, circuit breakers, and
  bulkheads.

The following specifications comprise the top layer of MicroProfile specifications:

- **Metrics** (https://microprofile.io/project/eclipse/
  microprofile-metrics): The Metrics specification provides a
  standard way to expose performance-related data from your
  application. This data can then be used to monitor your application.
  It also provides APIs for exporting metrics to monitoring systems.

- **Open Tracing** (https://microprofile.io/project/eclipse/
  microprofile-opentracing): The Open Tracing specification
  enables you to trace requests as they flow through your microservices
  architecture. It also provide APIs for tracing requests across
  microservices. This can be useful for debugging and performance
  analysis.

- **Health** (https://microprofile.io/project/eclipse/
  microprofile-health): The Health specification provides a standard
  way to expose health-related information from your application. This
  information can be used to monitor the health of your application. It
  provides APIs for writing health checks.

The Eclipse MicroProfile platform allows developers to choose the specifications they need for their microservices. It is also designed to be easily extended so that developers can add more features as needed. If a developer needs a new specification, they can request it from the MicroProfile community. If it's approved by the community, the new specification will be created and added to the MicroProfile platform in a future release. This makes the platform versatile and adaptable to any organization's needs.

Popular Implementations of the Eclipse MicroProfile Framework

The Eclipse MicroProfile is an essential tool for developers who want to create microservices. It provides a standard set of specifications that can be used to build microservices. This makes it easier for developers to share code and create interoperable services. Here are some of the popular implementations of MicroProfile:

- **Payara Micro** (https://www.payara.fish/products/payara-micro/): Payara Micro is the open-source, lightweight middleware platform of choice for developers, architects, and IT organizations looking to improve application server startups in production environments while providing a consistent development experience.

- **WildFly** (https://www.wildfly.org/): WildFly is a lightweight Jakarta EE-compliant application server.

- **Apache TomEE** (https://tomee.apache.org/): TomEE, pronounced "Tommy," is an all-Apache stack-aimed application server for Jakarta EE specifications.

- **Open Liberty** (https://openliberty.io/): Open Liberty is a fast, lightweight application server with a minimal footprint that supports Jakarta EE specifications.

- **Quarkus** (https://quarkus.io/): Quarkus is a Kubernetes-native Java stack tailored for GraalVM and OpenJDK HotSpot, crafted from the best-of-breed Java libraries and standards.

- **Helidon.io** (https://helidon.io/): Helidon is a microservices-based framework for developing Java applications.

- **Launcher** (`https://github.com/fujitsu/launcher`): Fujitsu launcher is a microservices-based application server.

- **KumuluzEE** (`https://ee.kumuluz.com/`): KumuluzEE is an open-source framework that simplifies the development of cloud-native applications written in Java.

In this book, I primarily use Open Liberty for demonstration, as it implements the latest MicroProfile standard. The development process should be similar if you want to use any other application server that supports Eclipse MicroProfile.

MicroProfile Config

A MicroProfile Config component provides APIs that help you manage your application's configuration. The Config API allows you to:

- Read and write configuration values

- Access configuration values from multiple sources, including property files, system properties, and environment variables

- Observe changes to configuration values using config events

Some of the features of the Config API include:

- `Config`: The `Config` class is used to access the configuration data.

- `ConfigSource`: A `ConfigSource` is used to read configuration data from a specific source.

- `Property`: A `Property` is used to represent a key/value pair in the configuration data.

- `Converter`: A `Converter` is used to convert between types in the configuration data.

- `Filter`: A `Filter` is used to filter the configuration data.

Maven Dependency

To use the Config API, you need to include the following dependency in your `pom.xml` file:

```
<dependency>
  <groupId>org.eclipse.microprofile.config</groupId>
    <artifactId>microprofile-config-api</artifactId>
    <version>1.0</version>
</dependency>
```

Enabling MicroProfile Config in Open Liberty

To enable the MicroConfig feature, you need to add the following code to the server.
xml file:

```
<featureManager>
<feature>mpConfig-1.4</feature>
</featureManager>
```

Working with MicroProfile Config

The Config class provides static methods that can be used to access configuration
properties. With the dependency in place, you can create a class called MyConfig that
looks like this:

```
import org.eclipse.microprofile.config.inject.ConfigProperty;

import jakarta.enterprise.context.ApplicationScoped;
import jakarta.inject.Inject;
import jakarta.inject.Named;

@ApplicationScoped
public class MyConfig {

    @Inject
    @ConfigProperty(name = "greeting",  defaultValue="Hello")
    private String greeting;

    public String getGreeting() {
        return greeting;
    }
}
```

The property file can be placed in the classpath or on the filesystem with the greeting.properties filename.

Defining the Config Property

The following is the source code for a property file that will be used to configure the greeting property:

```
greeting=Hello Microservices!
```

The MyConfig class is a standard Java class annotated with @ApplicationScoped, which means it will be created once and used for the lifetime of the application. The class has a single field annotated with @Inject and @ConfigProperty. The ConfigProperty annotation tells the Config API to inject the value of the greeting property into the field. If the property is not found, the default value of Hello will be used.

Testing the Config Component

The getGreeting() method simply returns the value of the greeting field. You can test this class by creating a RESTful web service endpoint that uses it:

```java
import jakarta.inject.Inject;
import jakarta.ws.rs.GET;
import jakarta.ws.rs.Path;
import jakarta.ws.rs.Produces;
import jakarta.ws.rs.core.MediaType;

@Path("/config")
public class ConfigResource {

    @Inject
    private MyConfig myConfig;

    @GET
    @Produces(MediaType.TEXT_PLAIN)
    public String getGreeting() {
        return myConfig.getGreeting();
    }
}
```

When you deploy the application and invoke the /config endpoint, you should see the greeting property that you injected:

```
Hello Microservices!
```

You can also inject configuration properties into parameter of a method, as shown here:

```
import org.eclipse.microprofile.config.inject.ConfigProperty;
// ...
public class MyConfig {

// ...


@Inject
public void setGreeting(@ConfigProperty(name = "greeting") String greeting)
```

Creating a ConfigSource

As you can see, the Config API makes it easy to inject configuration properties into an application. The Config API defines a contract for config implementations. A ConfigSource is used to read configuration data from a particular source. For example, you could create a ConfigSource that reads configuration data from a file.

The ConfigSource interface has the following methods:

- String getName(): Returns the name of the ConfigSource.

- int getOrdinal(): Returns the ordinal of the ConfigSource. Ordinals determine the precedence of ConfigSources. A higher ordinal means a higher precedence.

- Map<String, String> getProperties(): Returns a map of the properties in this ConfigSource. The keys in the map are the property names, and the values are the property values.

- getValue(String propertyName): Returns the value of the given property. If the property is not found, this method returns null.

- Set getPropertyNames(): Returns a Set of the property names in this ConfigSource.

The following is a simple implementation of a ConfigSource that reads configuration data from a file:

```java
import org.eclipse.microprofile.config.spi.ConfigSource;

import java.io.IOException;
import java.util.HashMap;
import java.util.Map;
import java.util.Set;

public class MyConfigSource implements ConfigSource {

    private Map<String, String> properties;

    public MyConfigSource() throws IOException {
        properties = new HashMap<>();
        properties.put("greeting", "Hello from MyConfigSource!");
    }

    public Map<String, String> getProperties() {
        return properties;
    }

    public String getValue(String propertyName) {
        return properties.get(propertyName);
    }

    public String getName() {
        return "MyConfigSource";
    }

    public Set<String> getPropertyNames() {
        return properties.keySet();
    }

    public int getOrdinal() {
        // we want this config source to have a higher precedence, so we
        return 1000
        return 1000;
    }
}
```

Reminder all source code is available from github.com/apress/ beginning-cloud-native-dev-microprofile-jakarta-kubernetes.

Registering a ConfigSource

Once you have implemented a ConfigSource, you need to register it with the Config API. You can do this by creating a file called org.eclipse.microprofile.config.spi. ConfigSource in the META-INF/services directory of your application. This file contains the fully qualified class name of your ConfigSource.

Accessing Configuration Data

Once your ConfigSource is registered, you can access the configuration data:

```
import org.eclipse.microprofile.config.Config;
public class MyApplication {
    // ...
    public void doSomething() {
        Config config = ConfigProvider.getConfig();
        String myProp = config.getValue("my.prop", String.class);
    }
}
```

This example uses the getValue() method to retrieve a property from ConfigSource. The first argument is the name of the property, and the second argument is the type that you want the property to be converted to. If the property does not exist, the default value (null in this case) will be returned. ConfigSources are hierarchical, which means that you can override properties from one ConfigSource with another ConfigSource. For example, you could create a ConfigSource that reads configuration data from a file and another ConfigSource that reads configuration data from system properties. The system properties would take precedence over the file-based ConfigSource, which would take precedence over the default ConfigSource.

Accessing Configuration Metadata

In addition to injecting configuration values into an application, the Config API also provides a way to access metadata about configuration properties. The Config interface uses the getProperty(String propertyName) method to access this metadata. It returns information about the given property. If the property is not found, this method returns null.

Specifying Default Values for the Config Property

You can also specify a default value to use if the property does not exist:

```
import org.eclipse.microprofile.config.inject.ConfigProperty;
public class MyApplication {
    @Inject
    @ConfigProperty(name="my.prop", defaultValue="foo")
    private String myProp;
}
```

In this example, the "foo" default value will be used if the my.prop property does not exist.

Type Conversion in a ConfigProperty

ConfigProperty also supports type conversion, so you can inject your configuration data into fields of any type:

```
import org.eclipse.microprofile.config.inject.ConfigProperty;
public class MyApplication {
    @Inject
    @ConfigProperty(name="my.prop", defaultValue="1234")
    private Integer myProp;
}
```

In this example, the my.prop property will be converted to an integer before it is injected into the myProp field. If the conversion fails, a org.eclipse.microprofile.config.ConversionFailedException will be thrown.

Using an Optional ConfigProperty

If you want your property to be injected as an optional field, you can use the org.
eclipse.microprofile.config.inject.ConfigProperty annotation:

```
import org.eclipse.microprofile.config.inject.ConfigProperty;
public class MyApplication {
    @Inject
    @ConfigProperty(name="my.prop")
    private Optional<String> myProp;
}
```

In this example, the myProp field will be injected with an Optional<String> object. If the property does not exist, the injected Optional will be empty. The optional properties are retrieved by the getOptionalValue() method instead of by getValue().

Converting Configuration Data Into a POJO

You can also use the Config API to convert the configuration data into a POJO:

```
import org.eclipse.microprofile.config.inject.ConfigProperty;
public class MyApplication {
    @Inject
    private MyPojo myPojo;
}
public class MyPojo {
    @ConfigProperty(name="my.prop")
    private String myProp;
}
```

This example is injecting a property named my.prop into the myProp field of the MyPojo class. If the property does not exist, a org.eclipse.microprofile.config.ConfigPropertyNotFoundException will be thrown. The code also shows how to access metadata about configuration properties and convert configuration data into a POJO.

Programmatically Looking Up Configuration Data

In addition to injection, you can also use the Config API to programmatically look up configuration data:

```
import org.eclipse.microprofile.config.inject.ConfigProperty;

public class MyApplication {
    public void doSomething() {
        Config config = ConfigProvider.getConfig();
        String myProp = config.getValue("my.prop", String.class);
    }
}
```

Like you can with injected fields, you can specify a default value to use if the property does not exist:

```
import org.eclipse.microprofile.config.inject.ConfigProperty;

public class MyApplication {
    public void doSomething() {
        Config config = ConfigProvider.getConfig();
        String myProp = config.getValue("my.prop");
    }
}
```

You can also use type conversion:

```
import org.eclipse.microprofile.config.inject.ConfigProperty;

public class MyApplication {
    public void doSomething() {
        Config config = ConfigProvider.getInstance().getConfig();
        Integer myProp = config.getValue("my.prop");
    }
}
```

The MicroProfile Health Check Specification

The Eclipse MicroProfile Health Check specification provides a set of annotations and APIs for writing health checks for your applications. A *health check* is a test that can be used to determine the health of an application or service. Some of the features of the Health Check component include:

- HealthCheck: Used to mark a class as a health checker.

- HealthCheckResponse: Used to represent the result of a health check.

- HealthCheckRegistry: Used to register and run health checkers.

The Health Check API allows you to expose information about the health of your application. This information can be used by load balancers and other tools to determine whether an application is healthy. To use the Health Check API, you need to include the following dependency in your pom.xml file:

```
<dependency>
<groupId>org.eclipse.microprofile.health</groupId>
<artifactId>microprofile-health-api</artifactId>
<version>1.0</version>
</dependency>
```

The Health Check API defines a contract for health check implementations. A health check is a Java class that implements the HealthCheck interface:

```
package org.eclipse.microprofile.health;

public interface HealthCheck {
    HealthCheckResponse call();
}
```

The call() method is used to perform the actual health check and return a HealthCheckResponse object:

```
package org.eclipse.microprofile.health;

public interface HealthCheckResponse {
  boolean isHealthy();
  String getMessage();
}
```

The isHealthy() method returns true if the health check was successful and false otherwise. The getMessage() method can be used to return a message describing the result of the health check.

You can create a health check by implementing the HealthCheck interface:

```
import org.eclipse.microprofile.health.Health;
import org.eclipse.microprofile.health.HealthCheck;
import org.eclipse.microprofile.health.HealthCheckResponse;

@Health
public class MyHealthCheck implements HealthCheck {

  @Override
  public HealthCheckResponse call() {
    return HealthCheckResponse.named("my-health-check")
        .withData("time", System.currentTimeMillis())
        .up()
        .build();
  }
}
```

The MyHealthCheck class is annotated with the @Health annotation, which tells the runtime that it is a health check. The call() method returns a HealthCheckResponse object, which indicates that the health check was successful and includes some data about the time the check was made.

You can deploy the application and invoke the /health endpoint to see the result of the health check:

```
{
  "status": "UP",
  "checks": [
    {
      "name": "my-health-check",
      "data": {
        "time": 1484648754368
      }
    }
  ]
}
```

As you can see, the health check was successful and the response includes the data that you specified in the health check. This next section looks at how to use the Fault Tolerance API to make your application more resilient to failure.

The MicroProfile Fault Tolerance Component

Fault tolerance is the ability of a system to continue operating correctly in the event of a failure. A fault-tolerant system is one that can detect, isolate, and recover from errors without human intervention.

Key Features of the Fault Tolerance Component

Some of the key features of the Fault Tolerance component include:

- **Circuit breaker**: A circuit breaker is used to prevent an application from making too many unsuccessful requests to a downstream system. If the number of failures exceeds a threshold, the circuit breaker will "open" and all subsequent requests will fail immediately. After a configured delay, the circuit breaker will "half-open" and allow a limited number of requests to go through. If those requests are successful, the circuit breaker will "close" and allow all requests to go through.

- **Bulkhead**: A bulkhead is used to isolate failures in one part of a system from other parts of the system. For example, if you have a system with a database and a web frontend, you can use a bulkhead to ensure that the database failures do not affect the web frontend.

- **Retry**: The system should retry an operation if it fails.

- **Timeout**: The timeout feature is used to abort an operation if it takes too long.

- **Fallback**: The fallback feature is used to provide a default response if an operation fails.

- **Asynchronous execution**: The system can execute operations asynchronously so that the caller does not have to wait for the operation to complete.

Fault Tolerance API

The Fault Tolerance API allows you to make your application more resilient to failures. This section looks at how to use the Fault Tolerance component to build a simple fault-tolerant application. Since fault tolerance is built on top of the Config API, you can use configuration data to configure the behavior of your fault-tolerant applications.

To use the Fault Tolerance API, you need to include the following dependency in your pom.xml file:

```
<dependency>
<groupId>org.eclipse.microprofile.faulttolerance</groupId>
<artifactId>microprofile-fault-tolerance-api</artifactId>
<version>1.0</version>
</dependency>
```

The Fault Tolerance API defines a contract for fault-tolerance implementations. A fault-tolerance annotation is used to annotate a Java method:

```
import org.eclipse.microprofile.faulttolerance.Retry;

@Retry(maxRetries = 3, delay = 1000)
public String doSomething() {
    // ...
}
```

The Retry annotation tells the runtime to retry the method up to three times when it fails. The Delay attribute specifies the amount of time to wait between retries, in milliseconds. If the method still fails after three attempts, the runtime will throw a FaultToleranceException.

The other fault-tolerance annotations are listed in Table 6-1.

Table 6-1. *Fault-Tolerance Annotations and Their Descriptions*

Fault-Tolerance Annotations	Descriptions
@Timeout	Specifies a timeout for the method. If the method takes longer than the specified timeout, it will be aborted and a FaultToleranceException will be thrown.
@CircuitBreaker	Specifies that the method should be executed in a circuit breaker. If the method fails too many times, the circuit breaker will open and the method will not be executed. After a period of time, the circuit breaker will close and the method will be executed again.
@Fallback	Specifies a fallback method to execute if the primary method fails.
@Bulkhead	Specifies that the method should be executed in a bulkhead. A bulkhead limits the number of concurrent executions of the method. If the limit is reached, subsequent calls to the method will be rejected.

These annotations can be combined to create more sophisticated fault-tolerance policies. For example, you could annotate a method with both Timeout and Fallback annotations:

```
import org.eclipse.microprofile.faulttolerance.Timeout;
import org.eclipse.microprofile.faulttolerance.Fallback;

@Timeout(1000)
@Fallback(MyFallbackMethod.class)
public String doSomething() {
    // ...
}
```

In this example, if the method takes longer than 1000 milliseconds to execute, it will be aborted and the fallback method will be executed.

Summary

This chapter looked at the MicroProfile Config and Fault Tolerance components. The next chapter covers using the Metrics component, building RESTful web services, generating documentation for the APIs using the Open API component, and using the OpenTracing component to trace your requests.

CHAPTER 7

MicroProfile Framework – Part 2

In the last chapter, you were introduced to MicroProfile's architecture. That chapter also covered a few essential standards in-depth, like configuration, health checking, and fault tolerance.

This chapter discusses some of the more critical standards in MicroProfile: Metrics, RESTful web services, open tracing, and the OpenAPI specification (OAS).

Metrics and health checking are two ways of monitoring the status of a service or application. While health checks can tell you whether a service is healthy, metrics provide information about the performance of a service. Let's now go through the MicroProfile Metrics specification in detail.

The MicroProfile Metrics Specification

The MicroProfile Metrics project provides a set of annotations and APIs for measuring the performance of your applications. It is a specification for exposing application metrics in a standard format. It allows other tools and frameworks to collect and track an application's metrics easily.

In other words, this specification defines a set of standard metrics that you can use to track the health and performance of an application. You can expose these metrics in various ways, such as using JMX, JSON, or Prometheus.

JMX is a Java Management Extension. It is a Java platform that provides tools for managing and monitoring Java applications. JMX can be used to monitor the performance of applications and to identify and diagnose problems.

The Prometheus tool is a monitoring and time-series database system. It allows you to collect metrics from your services and store them for long-term analysis.

© Tarun Telang 2023
T. Telang, *Beginning Cloud Native Development with MicroProfile, Jakarta EE, and Kubernetes*,
https://doi.org/10.1007/978-1-4842-8832-0_7

Types of Metrics

The MicroProfile Metrics specification defines a set of standard metrics; it can be divided into multiple categories:

- **Base metrics:** Common to all applications, such as the number of CPUs or the amount of free memory.

- **Application metrics**: Specific to an application, such as the number of requests per second or the average response time.

- **Vendor metrics**: Specific to a particular vendor or technology, such as the number of database queries per second.

In addition to the standard metrics mentioned here, MicroProfile Metrics also allows for custom metrics. You can use custom metrics to track application-specific information not covered by the standard metrics.

Metrics Components

Here are some of the essential Metrics components:

- `MetricRegistry`: Holds all the metrics for your application.

- `Meters`: Measure the rate at which an event occurs.

- `Gauges`: Measure the value of a function at a given point in time.

- `Counter`: Increments or decrements a value.

- `Histograms`: Track the distribution of values in a stream of data.

- *Timers*: Measure the time it takes to perform an operation.

The Metrics component also includes a JMX interface for exposing the metrics of your application.

Metrics Annotations

The MicroProfile Metrics spec defines a set of annotations to be used for exposing metrics. These annotations can be used on classes, methods, or fields. Table 7-1 lists the Metrics annotations along with their descriptions.

Table 7-1. Metrics Annotations

Annotation	Descriptions
@Timed	Determines how long a method takes to execute and exposes this information as a metric.
@Counted	Keeps track of the number of times a method is invoked and exposes this information as a metric.
@Gauge	Allows you to expose a custom metric that can be any value. It is useful for exposing application-specific metrics.
@ConcurrentGauge	Similar to the Gauge annotation, but allows tracking concurrent invocations of a method.
@Metered	Determines how long a method takes to execute and exposes this information as a rate metric.
@SimplyTimed	Determines how long a method takes to execute and exposes this information as both a total time metric and a rate metric

In addition to the annotations, the MicroProfile Metrics spec also defines a set of programmatic APIs for working with metrics. These APIs can be used to register custom metrics or to access existing metrics.

Maven Dependency

To use the Metrics component, you need the following Maven dependency:

```
<dependency>
    <groupId>org.eclipse.microprofile</groupId>
    <artifactId>microprofile-metrics</artifactId>
</dependency>
```

Tracking Response Time Using @Timed

The MicroProfile Metrics spec also allows you to track the response time of a method as a timed metric. The following code example shows how to use the @Timed annotation to track the response time.

```
import org.eclipse.microprofile.metrics.MetricType;
import org.eclipse.microprofile.metrics.annotation.Timed;

public class MyApplication {

    // Expose the response time as a timed metric
    @Timed(name = "responseTime", description = "The response time of the
    method", unit = "ms", metricType = MetricType.TIMER)
    public void myMethod() {
        // Method implementation
        // ....
    }
}
```

This will expose a metric called `myTimer`, which will track the amount of time spent in the `myMethod()` method in milliseconds.

Tracking the Number of Invocations

The MicroProfile Metrics spec also allows you to track the number of invocations of a method as a counter metric. The following code example shows how to use the `@Metric` annotation to track the invocation count:

```
import org.eclipse.microprofile.metrics.Metrics;
import org.eclipse.microprofile.metrics.MetricType;

public class MyApplication {
    // Expose the invocation count as a counter metric
    @Metric(name = "invocationCount", description = "The number of times
    the method has been invoked", unit = "invocations", metricType =
    MetricType.COUNTER)
    public int myMethod() {
        // Method implementation
        // ....
    }
}
```

In this example, the @Metric annotation tells MicroProfile Metrics to track the number of invocations of the myMethod() method and expose this metric as a counter. The name, description, and unit of the metric can also be specified. The metricType attribute is used to specify the type of metric, which in this case is a counter.

Tracking Memory Usage

You can also use MicroProfile Metrics to track the memory usage of your application. The following code example shows how to use the MicroProfile Metrics annotations to track the memory usage of a method:

```
import org.eclipse.microprofile.metrics.annotation.Metered;

public class MyApplication {
    // Track the memory usage of the method
    @Metered(name = "memoryUsage", unit = MetricUnits.BYTES, description
    = "The memory usage of the method in bytes", metricType = MetricType.
    METERED)
    public void myMethod() {
        // Method implementation
        // ....
    }
}
```

In this example, the @Metered annotation tells MicroProfile Metrics to track the memory usage of the myMethod() method and expose this metric as a meter. The name, description, and unit of the metric can also be specified.

MetricRegistry

The MetricRegistry is a registry of all metrics that are exposed via MicroProfile Metrics. It can be used to programmatically access metric values or to register custom metrics.

To get a reference to the MetricRegistry, you can inject it, as follows:

```
@Inject
MetricRegistry registry;
```

You can then use the `MetricRegistry` to access any exposed metric. For example, to get the value of the `request-rate` metric, you use the following:

```
Double requestRate = registry.getMetrics().get("request-rate").
doubleValue();
```

Creating Custom Metrics

You can also create your own metrics by implementing the `org.eclipse.microprofile.metrics.Metric` interface. The following code example creates a custom metric that tracks the number of active users in the application:

```
import org.eclipse.microprofile.metrics.Metric;
import org.eclipse.microprofile.metrics.MetricUnits;

public class ActiveUsersMetric implements Metric {
    private int activeUsers;

    public void setActiveUsers(int activeUsers) {
        this.activeUsers = activeUsers;
    }

    public int getValue() {
        return activeUsers;
    }

    public String getName() {
        return "activeUsers";
    }

    public MetricType getType() {
        return MetricType.GAUGE;
    }

    public String getUnit() {
        return MetricUnits.NONE;
    }
}
```

In this example, the ActiveUsersMetric class implements the Metric interface. This class has a setActiveUsers() method that sets the number of active users, and a getValue() method that gets the current value of the metric. The name, type, and unit of the metric can also be specified.

You can register your custom metric with MicroProfile Metrics using the org. eclipse.microprofile.metrics.MetricsRegistry interface. The following code example shows how to register a custom metric with MicroProfile Metrics:

```
public class MyApplication {
    public static void main(String[] args) {
        // Create the MetricRegistry
        MetricRegistry registry = Metrics.getRegistry();

        // Create the custom metric
        ActiveUsersMetric activeUsersMetric = new ActiveUsersMetric();

        // Register the metric
        registry.register("activeUsers", activeUsersMetric);
    }
}
```

In this example, a custom MetricRegistry is created and the custom metric is registered with it. You can then use MetricRegistry to retrieve the value of the metric. For example, you could use the following code to get the value of the activeUsers metric:

```
int activeUsers = registry.getGaugeValue("activeUsers");
```

Exposing Metrics

JMX

To expose metrics via Java Management Extensions (JMX), add the following dependency to your project:

```
<dependency>
<groupId>org.eclipse.microprofile.metrics</groupId>
<artifactId>microprofile-metrics-api</artifactId>
<version>2.3</version>
</dependency>
```

This will enable JMX support for MicroProfile Metrics in your application. By default, all metrics are exposed via JMX. If you want to disable this, you can set the following property in your application's configuration:

```
mp.metrics.jmx.disabled=true
```

JSON

To expose metrics in JSON format, add the following dependency to your project:

```
<dependency>
<groupId>org.eclipse.microprofile.metrics</groupId>
<artifactId>microprofile-metrics-rest</artifactId>
<version>2.3</version>
</dependency>
```

This will enable JSON support for MicroProfile Metrics in your application. By default, all metrics are exposed in JSON format. If you want to disable this, you can set the following property in your application's configuration:

```
mp.metrics.rest.disabled=true
```

Prometheus

To expose metrics in Prometheus format, add the following dependency to your project:

```
<dependency>
    <groupId>org.eclipse.microprofile.metrics</groupId>
    <artifactId>microprofile-metrics-impl</artifactId>
    <version>2.3</version>
</dependency>
```

This will enable Prometheus support for MicroProfile Metrics in your application. By default, all metrics are exposed in Prometheus format.

If you want to disable this, you can set the following property in your application's configuration:

```
mp.metrics.prometheus.disabled=true
```

The MicroProfile Metrics spec is a useful tool for monitoring the performance of your application. It can be used to track the execution time of methods, the memory usage of methods, and custom metrics that you define. MicroProfile Metrics is easy to use and can be integrated with other monitoring tools.

Using Open Tracing

The MicroProfile OpenTracing specification defines a standard set of APIs for enabling distributed tracing in your methods. The goal of the MicroProfile OpenTracing specification is to maintain consistency across different tracing implementations, such as Jaeger (`www.jaegertracing.io/`), Zipkin (`https://zipkin.io/`), and AppDynamics (`www.appdynamics.com/`). This means that you can use any compatible tracing implementation with your microservices, without having to change your code.

The MicroProfile OpenTracing specification consists of two parts:

- The API definition describes how to instrument RESTful web services for distributed tracing.

- The compatibility layer allows different tracing implementations to be used interchangeably with the MicroProfile OpenTracing API.

Distributed Tracing

Distributed tracing is a technique for understanding how distributed systems work by tracing the flow of requests through the system. It is used to troubleshoot different kinds of issues, such as performance issues, and identify bottlenecks in distributed systems. In a microservices architecture, each microservice is a separate process that runs on its machine. Requests can flow from one microservice to another, so it can be difficult to understand how the system works as a whole.

Distributed tracing can help you see the big picture by tracing the flow of requests through the system and identifying which microservices are involved in each request.

How Does It Work?

The MicroProfile OpenTracing API defines how to instrument microservices for distributed tracing. The API is based on the OpenTracing standard, which is a vendor-neutral way of instrumenting distributed systems for tracing. Without distributed tracing, it can be difficult to understand how a request flows through a microservice architecture.

The MicroProfile OpenTracing compatibility layer allows different tracing implementations to be used with the MicroProfile OpenTracing API. This means that you can use any compatible tracing implementation with your microservices, without having to change your code.

MicroProfile OpenTracing Within a Jakarta RESTful Web Service

To implement OpenTracing, first you need to include the following Maven dependencies in the pom.xml file of your project.

```
<dependency>
  <groupId>org.eclipse.microprofile.opentracing</groupId>
  <artifactId>microprofile-opentracing-api</artifactId>
  <version>3.0</version>
</dependency>
```

To enable distributed tracing in your application with Zipkin, first ensure it is installed and running. Refer to Chapter 3 to learn about how to install Zipkin on your system. Next, add the following code to your server.xml file.

Assuming you are using Open Liberty as your MicroProfile implementation, the server.xml file will be located in the following path:

```
/<project-folder>/src/main/liberty/config
```

After your RESTful web services are running, you can look for the traces in your Zipkin server.

By default, all the methods in a Jakarta RESTful web service resources are traced. You can use the @Traced(false) annotation to exclude certain methods from being traced.

Explicitly Enabling OpenTracing

To enable tracing for non-Jakarta RESTful web service methods, you need to add the @Traced annotation to the method. Here is the code snippet for the same:

```
@Traced (value = true, operationName = "MyApplication.someMethod")
public void someMethod() {
    // ...
}
```

The operationName=<Span name> parameter specifies the name of the span.

Injecting a Custom Tracer Object

The underlying OpenTracing Tracer object can be injected into a Jakarta RESTful web service resource class using the @Inject annotation via CDI.

```
public class MyApplication {

    @Inject
    private Tracer tracer;

    public void someMethod() {
    // ... do something with the tracer
    }
}
```

After that, you can start to instrument your code by creating spans. For example, to instrument a method, do the following:

```
public class MyApplication {

    private Tracer tracer;

    public void someMethod() {
        Span span = tracer.buildSpan("someOperation").start();

        try (Scope scope = tracer.scopeManager().activate(span)){
            // ... do something here

        } finally {
            span.finish();

        }
    }
}
```

The finish() method is called in a finally block to ensure that the span is always completed, even if an exception is thrown. It sets the status and end time of the span.

Logs can be used to add information about events that happen during the span, by using the span.log() method.

You can also add tags to the span by using the `tracer.setTag()` method:

```
public class MyApplication {

private Tracer tracer;

    public void someMethod() {
        Span span = tracer.buildSpan("someOperation").start();

        try (Scope scope = tracer.scopeManager().activate(span)){
            // ... do something here
            span.log("something happened here");
            span.setTag("operationType", "read");

            // ... do something here
        } finally {
            span.finish();
        }
    }
}
```

For more information, refer to the MicroProfile OpenTracing specification (https://download.eclipse.org/microprofile/microprofile-opentracing-3.0/microprofile-opentracing-spec-3.0.html).

Using the Jakarta RESTful Web Service

Web services are very popular nowadays because they allow for building decoupled systems, whereby services can communicate with each other without the knowledge of each other's implementation details.

There are many ways to design and implement web services. One popular way is to use the Representational State Transfer (REST) architecture.

A Jakarta RESTful web service uses the REST architecture. This type of web service makes it easy to build modern, scalable web applications. The REST architecture is based on the principle that all data and functionality should be accessed through a uniform interface. This makes it easy to develop, test, and deploy web applications.

For example, let's say you have a product catalog that you want to make available as a web service. With REST, you create an URL that represents the resources (products) in your catalog. When a client (such as a web browser) requests this URL, the server will return a list of products in JSON format.

Let's create this simple RESTful web service. To use Jakarta RESTful web services APIs, you need to add the following Maven dependency to your project:

```
<!-- https://mvnrepository.com/artifact/jakarta.ws.rs/jakarta.ws.rs-api -->
<dependency>
    <groupId>jakarta.ws.rs</groupId>
    <artifactId>jakarta.ws.rs-api</artifactId>
    <version>3.1.0</version>
</dependency>
```

Now define the Product class as a POJO:

```
public class Product {
    private int id;
    private String name;

    public String getName() {
        return name;
    }

    public int getId() {
        return id;
    }

    public Product(int id, String name) {
        this.id = id;
        this.name = name;
    }
}
```

Next, create a `ProductService` class with a `getProducts()` method, which returns a list of products:

```
import java.util.*;
import jakarta.ws.rs.*;
@Path("/products")
public class ProductService {
    @GET
    @Produces(MediaType.APPLICATION_JSON)
    public List<Product> getProducts() {
        // Return a list of products
        List<Product> products = new ArrayList<>();

        products.add(new Product(1, " product 1"));
        products.add(new Product(2, "product 2"));

        return products;
    }
}
```

You also need to create an `Application`:

```
import jakarta.ws.rs.ApplicationPath;
import jakarta.ws.rs.core.Application;

@ApplicationPath("/api")
public class HelloApplication extends Application {

}
```

This class will be used to configure the JAX-RS application. The `@ApplicationPath` annotation defines the base URI for all resources in this application.

You can then deploy this application on a Jakarta EE-compliant server and access the web service at `http://localhost:8080/api/products`. You should see a list of products in JSON format as shown here:

```
[{"id":1,"name":"product_1"},{"id":2,"name":"product_2"}]
```

Using the MicroProfile OpenAPI Specification

The MicroProfile OpenAPI specification provides a set of Java APIs that allow developers to define and auto-generate API specifications based on OpenAPI v3 standards from their RESTful web services. These API specifications can then be used to generate interactive documentation, client SDKs, and other tools that make it easier for developers to consume MicroProfile-based APIs.

The MicroProfile OpenAPI is part of the Eclipse MicroProfile project and is compatible with all major MicroProfile implementations. It is based on the OpenAPI Specification (OAS) and uses annotations from the Jakarta RESTful web services specification. In particular, the MicroProfile OpenAPI specification defines how to describe REST APIs that use JSON over HTTP.

OpenAPI

The OpenAPI Specification, formerly Swagger, is a technical specification for describing and documenting the interface between REST APIs and their consumers. It allows REST API providers to describe and expose their APIs using a format that can be consumed by a variety of tools. This facilitates the creation of APIs that are consistent, well-documented, and easily consumable by both humans and machines. The specification aims to provide a uniform way of describing APIs so that they are both human-readable and machine-readable. The OAS3 Specification is a community-driven initiative and is used by many large organizations, including Google, Microsoft, and Amazon.

Capabilities of the MicroProfile OpenAPI Specification

MicroProfile OpenAPI allows developers to easily generate documentation for their microservices. The documentation includes information on what services are provided, how to invoke them, and what data types are used. In addition, the documentation can be used to generate client code that can be used to access the web services.

Generating OpenAPI Documents

There are multiple ways that you can generate OpenAPI documents. The most common way is to use annotations. This only requires augmenting your existing Jakarta RESTful web services annotations with OpenAPI annotations.

You can also use JSON or YAML files. You can start with a predefined model and manually update the entire OpenAPI document tree for your web services. However, the annotation-based approach is the recommended one, as it is more maintainable and easier to understand. Finally, you can filter out the resources that you do not want to document using configuration.

Using the MicroProfile OpenAPI in Your Project

To use the MicroProfile OpenAPI in your project, you need to add the following Maven coordinates to your project:

```
<dependency>
        <groupId>org.eclipse.microprofile.openapi</groupId>
        <artifactId>microprofile-openapi-api</artifactId>
        <version>3.1-RC1</version>
        <type>jar</type>
</dependency>
```

This dependency contains the annotations that you need to document your API.

First, you need to create a Jakarta RESTful web service resource class that contains the API methods that you want to document:

```
import jakarta.ws.rs.GET;
import jakarta.ws.rs.Path;
import jakarta.ws.rs.Produces;
import jakarta.ws.rs.core.MediaType;
import java.util.List;

@Path("/myresource")
public class MyResource {

    @GET
    @Produces(MediaType.APPLICATION_JSON)
    @Operation(summary = "Get all MyObjects")
    @APIResponse(responseCode = "200", description = " successful
    operation",
                content = @Content(schema = @Schema(implementation =
                MyObject.class))),
```

```
@APIResponse(responseCode = "400", description = "MyObject not found")
public List <MyObject> getAll() {
    // ...
}
```
}

This example has a resource class with a single API method, getAll(). This method returns a list of MyObjects.

This method is annotated with the @Operation annotation to document the operation on a resource. The summary field provides a brief description of the operation.

The getAll() method is annotated with the @APIResponse annotation to document the successful response from the operation. The responseCode field specifies the status code of the response, and the description field provides a brief description of the response. There are two possible responses—a successful response containing a list of MyObjects with a 200 status code, and an unsuccessful response with a 400 status code, if no MyObjects are found. The content field specifies the schema of the response content. In this example, the response content is a list of MyObjects.

Finally, you need to add the following property to the src/main/resources/META-INF/microprofile-config.properties file:

mp.openapi.scan=true

This property tells the MicroProfile OpenAPI to scan your classes for annotations and generate API documentation for them.

Now that you have configured the MicroProfile OpenAPI, you can build and run your application.

When you access the http://localhost:8080/openapi.json URL, you should see the API documentation that was generated by the MicroProfile OpenAPI:

```
{
  "openapi": "3.0.1",
  "info": {
    "version": "1.0.0",
    "title": "My API"
  },
  "paths": {
    "/myresource": {
```

```
      "get": {
        "operationId": "getAll",
        "summary": "Get all MyObjects",
        "responses": {
          "200": {
            "description": " successful operation",
            "content": {
              "application/json": {
                "schema": {
                  "$ref": "#/components/schemas/MyObject"
                }
              }
            }
          },
          "400": {
            "description": "Invalid input"
          }
        }
      }
    }
  },
  "components": {
    "schemas": {
      "MyObject": {
        "type": "object",
        "properties": {},
        "javaType": "com.example.MyObject"
      }
    }
  }
}
```

As you can see, the MicroProfile OpenAPI has generated API documentation for this resource class. You can use this documentation to learn about the API and how to use it.

MicroProfile OpenAPI Annotations

The MicroProfile OpenAPI annotations can be used to document any Jakarta RESTful web services resource. The annotations can also be used in conjunction with other Jakarta RESTful web services annotations, such as @Path and @Produces. The annotations commonly used to document RESTful web services are listed in Table 7-2.

Table 7-2. *Annotations Used in the MicroProfile OpenAPI*

Annotation	Details
@OpenAPIDefinition	Used to define general information about the API, such as the title, description, version, etc.
@Operation	Used to document an operation on a resource. The summary and description fields provide a summary and description of the operation.
@Parameter	Used to document a parameter for an operation.
@Tag	Used to document a tag for an operation or resource. The name field specifies the name of the tag, and the description field provides a description of the tag.
@APIResponse	Used to document a response from an operation.
@RequestBody	Used to document the request body for an operation.

All of these annotations are defined in the org.eclipse.microprofile.openapi. annotations package.

Summary

In this chapter, you learned most of the essential concepts related to the MicroProfile framework. In the next chapter, you see how to secure a RESTful web service using the JWT propagation feature of MicroProfile.

CHAPTER 8

MicroProfile JSON Web Tokens and Jakarta Security

This chapter discusses the MicroProfile JSON Web Token specification. It first covers an overview of a JWT and then discusses the specifics of the MicroProfile implementation. Finally, the chapter includes some code examples for how to use JWT in a microservice environment.

Security Best Practices for Microservices

Microservices are all the rage these days. But with more services comes more complexity—and with more complexity comes a greater risk of security breaches. So how do you go about securing your microservices?

There are a few basic steps you can take to get started. First, make sure that each service is properly authenticated and authorized. Second, use encryption to protect sensitive data as it moves between services. Third, employ robust monitoring and logging tools to detect and track suspicious activity. And finally, be sure to keep your software up-to-date with the latest security patches.

Following these steps will help you secure your microservices against the most common attacks, but it's important to stay vigilant and always watch for new threats.

Let's now look into controlling user and role access to microservices with MicroProfile JSON Web Token.

© Tarun Telang 2023
T. Telang, *Beginning Cloud Native Development with MicroProfile, Jakarta EE, and Kubernetes*,
https://doi.org/10.1007/978-1-4842-8832-0_8

What Is a JSON Web Token (JWT)?

A JSON Web Token or JWT is an open standard that defines a compact and self-contained way of securely transmitting information between parties as a JSON object. JWTs can represent any claim, such as identity, security roles, or session information. These claims can be verified and trusted because they are digitally signed. JWTs can be signed using a secret key or a public/private key pair. They can also be used for authorization by allowing users to access specific resources only if they have a valid JWT.

The MicroProfile JSON Web Token specification defines how JWTs can be used in a microservice environment, including how to verify and validate tokens. It builds on the JWT standard and adds some additional features that are specific to microservices.

Use Cases for JSON Web Tokens

JSON Web Tokens can be used in the following scenarios.

Authentication

JWTs can be used to authenticate users. A user can be authenticated by providing a JWT with the correct signature. In-memory authentication is faster and more convenient as user credentials are stored in memory, but it is less secure because the data is more vulnerable to attack. DB stored user credentials are slower and more challenging to use, but they are more secure because the data is better protected either by encrypting it or through access control. Encryption makes it more difficult for hackers to access and steal information. Access control ensures that only authorized users have permission to view or modify the data.

Authorization

One common use case for JSON Web Tokens is an authorization. In this scenario, the JWT contains claims representing the user's identity and security roles. These claims can determine what resources the user is allowed to access.

For example, a user with the admin security role might be allowed to access all resources. In contrast, a user with the read-only security role might only be allowed to access resources marked as readable.

Session Information

Another common use case for JSON Web Tokens is storing session information. In this scenario, the JWT contains claims representing the user's session information, such as when the session started and when it will expire. This information can track a user's session and ensure that it does not exceed a certain time limit.

Claims-Based Identity

JWTs can also be used to represent claims-based identity. In this scenario, the JWT contains claims representing the user's identity, such as their name and email address. These claims can be used by applications to identify the user.

For example, an application might use the user's email address claim to look up their profile information in a database. Or, an application might use the user's name claim to display the user's name on a welcome page.

JWTs can be used with other identity providers, such as LDAP or Active Directory, to provide a single sign-on experience for users.

Information Exchange

JWTs can also be used to exchange information between parties. In this scenario, the JWT contains claims representing the data being exchanged. For example, a JWT might contain an order ID claim and a user ID claim. These claims can be used by the application to look up the order and display it to the user.

JWTs can exchange information and are often used in single sign-on (SSO) systems.

Federation

JWTs can also be used in federation scenarios. In this scenario, the JWT contains claims representing the user's identity. These claims can be used by the application to identify the user and look up their profile information.

JWTs can be used with other identity providers, such as Active Directory Federation Services (ADFS), to provide a single sign-on experience for users.

Creating and Signing a JWT

A JWT consists of three parts: a header, a payload, and a signature. Each part is separated from the others by a dot:

sdfdfsdfsdSDFJJEOKJA.OdsfDNFSUJSDJ.ASDSAasdhjasS

The header and payload are JSON objects, and the signature is a digital signature that can be used to verify that the JWT has not been tampered with.

The *header* typically contains information about the algorithm used to sign the JWT, and the *payload* contains the actual claims. The claims can be anything you want to represent, such as the user's name, email address, or security role.

The header of a JWT contains the following information:

- The type of token (JWT)

- The algorithm used to create the signature (HS256)

Here is an example header and payload.

Header:

```
{
"typ": "JWT",
"alg": "HS256"
}
```

Payload:

```
{
"iss": "Bob",
"exp": 1463808400,
"http://example.com/is_root": true,
"sub": "alice"
}
```

In this example, the payload contains the following claims:

- iss: The issuer of the token

- exp: The expiration time of the token

- `http://example.com/is_root`: A flag indicating whether or not the token is for the root resource

- `sub`: The subject of the token

You should keep the token as short as possible. Don't add a lot of data to the body. If the token is too long, it slows the request.

The *signature* is generated by signing the header and payload with a secret key. This secret key is known only to the issuer of the JWT and helps ensure that the JWT has not been tampered with.

Here is an example of a JWT signature:

eyJhbGciOiJIUzI1NiIsInR5cCI6IkpXVCJ9.eyJuYW1lIjoicmVzb3VyY2UiLCJzdWIiOiJQ
cm9maWxlIiwianRpIjoibWFya2V0aW5nIl0sImdldENvcnJlY3RNc2ciOiJVc2VySGV4ZWN1d
Gl2ZSIsInNlcW5vIjoiZXhhbXBsZS1jbGljayIsImlzcyI6InNlcW5vIiwic2VyaWYiOiJVc2
VySGV4ZWN1dGl2ZSIsInR5cGUiOiJVc2VySGV4ZWN1dGl2ZSIsInNyYyIjoibWFya2V0aW5n
Il0sImFtciI6IlNlcW5vIl0sImdybybCI6IlNlcW5vIlo

To create and sign a JWT, you need a few things:

- A JSON object that contains the claims or assertions that you want to include in the JWT. This is also known as the payload.

- A secret key or a public/private key pair.

- An algorithm that will be used to sign the JWT.

The claims that you include in the payload will depend on your application. Some common claims are listed here:

- `iss` (issuer): The issuer of the JWT. This is typically the URL of the service that issued the JWT.

- `sub` (subject): The subject of the JWT. This is typically the user ID of the authenticated user.

- `aud` (audience): The audience for the JWT. This is typically the URL of the service that will consume the JWT.

- `exp` (expiration time): The expiration time of the JWT. This is used to prevent replay attacks.

- nbf (not before): The time before which the JWT must not be accepted for processing.

- iat (issued at): The time at which the JWT was issued.

- jti (JWT ID): A unique identifier for the JWT.

The code that creates and signs a JWT is shown here:

```java
import org.eclipse.microprofile.jwt.JsonWebToken;

import jakarta.enterprise.context.RequestScoped;
import jakarta.inject.Inject;
import java.util.HashMap;
import java.util.Map;

@RequestScoped
public class JWTGenerator {

    private static final Logger LOG = Logger.getLogger(JWTGenerator.
    class.getName());
    private static final String ISSUER = "https://example.com";

    @Inject
    private JsonWebToken jwt;

    public String generate() {
        LOG.log(Level.INFO, "Generating JWT for: {0}", jwt.getName());

        Map<String, Object> claims = new HashMap<>();
        claims.put("iss", ISSUER);
        claims.put("sub", jwt.getSubject());
        claims.put("aud", "https://example.com/resources");
        claims.put("exp", System.currentTimeMillis() + 60 * 1000); //
        1 minute

        return Jwts.builder().setClaims(claims).
        signWith(SignatureAlgorithm.HS512, "secret".getBytes()).
        compact();
    }
}
```

Explanation:

The JWTGenerator class is annotated with the RequestScoped annotation. This means that a new instance of this class will be created for each request. The JWTGenerator class has a generate method, which creates and signs a JWT.

The generate method injects the JsonWebToken interface. This interface provides access to information about the authenticated user, such as the user's name and ID.

The generate method creates a map, which is used to store the claims that will be included in the JWT. The iss (issuer), sub (subject), aud (audience), and exp (expiration time) claims are added to the map. The iss claim is set to the URL of the service that issued the JWT. The sub claim is set to the user ID of the authenticated user. The aud claim is set to the URL of the service that will consume the JWT. The exp claim is used to prevent replay attacks and is set to 1 minute from the current time.

The claims are used to create a JWT that's signed using the HS512 algorithm and a secret key. The signed JWT is then returned from the generate method.

Testing the Application

To test the application, you can use curl to make a request to the /resources/jwks endpoint. This endpoint will return the public key, which can be used to verify the signature of the JWT.

```
$ curl -i http://localhost:8080/resources/jwks
```

You should see the following response:

```
HTTP/1.1 200
Content-Type: application/json;charset=UTF-8
Content-Length: 779
```

```
{"keys":[{"kty":"RSA","e":"AQAB","use":"sig","kid":"jwk-rsa1","alg":"RS256"
,"n":"yNWVhtYEKJR21y9xsHV-PD_bYwbXSeNuFal46xYxVfRL5mqha7vttvjB_vc7Xg2RvgCxH
PCqoxgMPTzHrZT75LjCwIIaUl4-qazaG4ZoTxziTYjsBMvsPuUvMVQe
...
```

Verifying and Validating a JWT

To verify and validate a JWT, you need to have the secret key used to sign the JWT. This secret key is typically held by the issuer of the JWT. The signature is verified by signing the header and payload with the secret key and comparing the signature to the one in the JWT. If they match, the JWT is considered to be valid.

The claims in the payload are also validated to ensure they have not been tampered with. For example, the expiry time (exp) claim is checked to ensure that the JWT has not expired.

To validate the signature of a JWT, you need to configure a `SignatureConfiguration`. This can be done programmatically or via the MicroProfile Config.

The following is an example of how to configure a `SignatureConfiguration` programmatically:

```
SignatureConfiguration signatureConfig =
new SignatureConfiguration()
.setKeyId("jwt-key")
.setSignatureAlgorithm(SignatureAlgorithm.RS256)
.setKeyStoreLocation("/path/to/keystore.jks")
.setKeyStorePassword("secret");
```

This example uses an RSA256 signature algorithm and the keystore is located at /path/to/keystore.jks. The keystore password is "secret".

You can also configure the `SignatureConfiguration` via the MicroProfile Config:

```
mp.jwt.verify.signature.key-id=jwt-key
mp.jwt.verify.signature.algorithm=RS256
mp.jwt.verify.signature.key-store-location=/path/to/keystore.jks
mp.jwt.verify.signature.key-store-password=secret
```

Once you have your `SignatureConfiguration` set up, you can create a `JWTProcessor` and pass in your configuration:

```
JWTProcessor jwtProcessor = new DefaultJWTProcessor();
jwtProcessor.setSignatureConfiguration(signatureConfig);
```

Now that you have your `JWTProcessor` configured, you can use it to validate the signature of a JWT:

```
JWTClaimsSet claimsSet = jwtProcessor.process(jwtString, null);
```

If the signature is valid, the `process()` method will return a `JWTClaimsSet`. If the signature is invalid, an exception will be thrown.

Using JWT in a Microservice Environment

The MicroProfile JSON Web Token specification is an important part of the security of a microservice environment. In a microservice environment, each service is typically responsible for its security. This means that each service needs to be able to verify and validate JWTs.

JSON Web Token is a popular token format for microservices because it follows well-defined and known standards. A token-based authentication mechanism offers a lightweight way for security tokens to propagate user identities across different services.

The MicroProfile JSON Web Token specification defines how JWTs can be used in a microservice environment. The specification defines a set of claims that are specific to the needs of microservices. These claims include the issuer, subject, and audience of the token. In addition, the specification defines how JWT can be used in a microservice environment, including how to verify and validate tokens.

As an example of how to use JWT in a microservice environment, suppose you have two microservices—an auth service, and a product service. The auth service is responsible for authenticating users and issuing JWTs. The product service is responsible for managing users.

The auth service issues JWTs to users after they have authenticated. These JWTs contain claims about the users, such as their name and email address. The product service uses the MicroProfile JWT specification to verify and validate the JWTs issued by the auth service. The product service can then use the information in the JWTs to identify the users accessing it. Figure 8-1 depicts the sequence of steps taken to authenticate and fetch data from the product service.

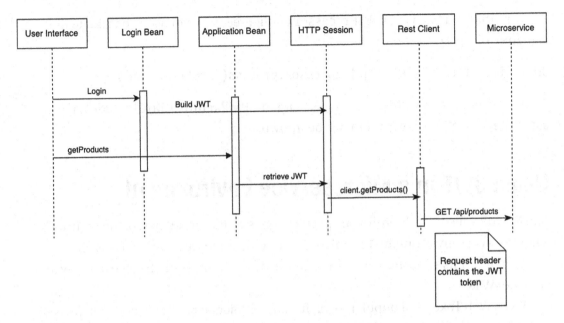

Figure 8-1. *Sequence diagram showing JWT propagation*

For more on JSON Web Token (JWT), visit the JWT website at `https://jwt.io`.

Securing a RESTful Application

Using the JWT feature in MicroProfile, you can secure your REST applications by specifying the following annotations:

```
@LoginConfig(authMethod = "MP-JWT", realmName = "jwt-jaspi")
@DeclareRoles({"user", "admin"})
public class MyApplication extends Application {

    // ...
}
```

The `MyApplication` class is secured with the `MP-JWT` authentication method and the `jwt-jaspi` realm. The `user` and `admin` roles are declared.

This example uses the `MP-JWT` feature to secure a REST application. You can also use it to secure other applications, such as Java EE web applications.

The complete code that secures the REST application is shown here:

```
import org.eclipse.microprofile.auth.LoginConfig;

import jakarta.annotation.security.DeclareRoles;
import jakarta.ws.rs.ApplicationPath;
import jakarta.ws.rs.core.Application;

@LoginConfig(authMethod = "MP-JWT", realmName = "jwt-jaspi")
@DeclareRoles({"user", "admin"})
@ApplicationPath("/")
public class MyApplication extends Application {
    // ...
}
```

The MyApplication class is also annotated with the LoginConfig and DeclareRoles annotations. The LoginConfig annotation configures the authentication method and realm name. This example uses the MP-JWT authentication method and the jwt-jaspi realm. The user and admin roles are declared.

Securing a REST Resource

The MicroProfile JWT API also defines a set of annotations for securing the REST resources. These annotations can be used to protect resources in a RESTful application. In Chapter 4, you learned about RESTful web services and the role of various HTTP methods.

The following code shows how to use the MicroProfile annotations to protect resources in a RESTful application:

```
import org.eclipse.microprofile.jwt.JWTAccessDeniedException;
import java.security.Principal;

import jakarta.annotation.security.DenyAll;
import jakarta.annotation.security.PermitAll;
import jakarta.annotation.security.RolesAllowed;
import jakarta.enterprise.context.RequestScoped;
import jakarta.inject.Inject;
import jakarta.ws.rs.container.ContainerRequestContext;
```

```java
import jakarta.ws.rs.core.Context;
import jakarta.ws.rs.core.SecurityContext;
import java.io.IOException;

@Path("/")
@RequestScoped
public class Resource {

    @Inject
    Principal caller;

    @Context
    SecurityContext securityContext;

    @GET
    public String doGet() {
        if (securityContext.isUserInRole("admin")) {
            return "admin";
        } else {
            return "user";
        }
    }

    // This resource is only accessible to users with the role "admin"
    @GET
    @Path("/admin")
    @RolesAllowed("admin")
    public String doGetAdmin() {
        return "admin";
    }

    // This resource is accessible to all users
    @GET
    @Path("/public")
    @PermitAll
    public String doGetPublic() {
        return "public";
    }
```

```
// This resource is not accessible to any user
@GET
@Path("/denied")
@DenyAll
public String doGetDenied() {
    return "denied";
}

public void displayUserDetails() {
        Principal principal = securityContext.getUserPrincipal();
        String name = principal.getName();
        // the "name" claim
        String email = principal.getClaim("email");
        // the "email" claim

        // ...
    }

}
```

In this example, the /admin resource is only accessible to users with the admin role. The /public resource is accessible to all users. The /denied resource is not accessible to any user.

The java.security.Principle interface can be used to get information about the caller from the JWT token. The displayUserDetails() method shows you how to use it to get information about the caller.

The @RolesAllowed Annotation

The @RolesAllowed can be used to protect resources in a RESTful application. The roles that are allowed to access the resource are specified in the annotation.

For example, suppose you have a RESTful resource that is only accessible to users with the admin role. This can be accomplished by annotating the resource with @RolesAllowed("admin").

The following code shows how to use the @RolesAllowed annotation to protect resources in a RESTful application. The roles allowed to access the resource are specified in the annotation.

```
@RestController
@RequestMapping("/users")
public class ProductResource {

@RolesAllowed("admin")
protected List<User> getProducts() {
        // get users from database here
}

...

}
```

In this example, only users with the admin role can call the getProducts() method of the Products resource.

The @Claim Annotation

The @Claim annotation can be used to inject the value of a claim into a Java method parameter. The name of the claim is specified in the annotation.

For example, suppose you have a method that needs to access the email address of the user making the request. This can be accomplished by annotating the email parameter with @Claim("email").

The following code shows how to use the @Claim annotation to inject the value of a claim into a Java method parameter. The name of the claim is specified in the annotation.

```
public void doSomething(@Claim("email") String email) {
        // do something with the email address here
}
```

In this example, the email address of the user is injected into the doSomething() method.

The @HeaderParam Annotation

The @HeaderParam annotation can inject the value of an HTTP header into a Java method parameter. The name of the header is specified in the annotation.

For example, suppose you have a method that needs to access the value of authHeader. This can be accomplished by annotating the header parameter with @HeaderParam("authHeader").

The following code shows how to use the @HeaderParam annotation to inject the value of an HTTP header into a Java method parameter. The name of the header is specified in the annotation.

```
public void doSomething(@HeaderParam("authHeader") String authHeader) {
    // do something with the authHeader here
}
```

In this example, the value of authHeader is injected into the doSomething method.

Configuring a JWK Set or PEM-Encoded Public Key

The MicroProfile JWT Auth specifications support the following public key formats:

- Public Key Cryptography Standards #8 in PEM Format

- JSON Web Key (JWK)

Public Key Cryptography Standards #8 in PEM Format

To configure a public key in PEM format, you need to set the following MicroProfile Config properties:

```
mp.jwt.verify.publickey.location=/META-INF/publicKey.pem
mp.jwt.verify.publickey.format=PEM
```

The value of the mp.jwt.verify.publickey.location property must be a path to the PEM-encoded public key file. The file can be located in the application's resources.

The following is an example of a PEM-encoded public key:

```
-----BEGIN PUBLIC KEY-----
MIICIjANBgkqhkiG9w0BAQEFAAOCAg8AMIICCgKCAgEAuYP6FyP/cTmVnxE1JXs+
5ySE+FNxztkOaDV8pPiwoZmxIkcH2QYP1XCfY16/mO5zt6nEJbDP7OiWl57bFmuG
KTPvfOHXlh17UfStys ...
-----END PUBLIC KEY-----
```

JSON Web Key (JWK)

A JSON Web Key (JWK) is a JavaScript Object Notation (JSON) data structure that represents a cryptographic key. A JWK Set is a JSON data structure representing a set of JWKs.

To configure a JWK Set, you need to set the following MicroProfile Config properties:

```
mp.jwt.verify.publickey.location=/META-INF/jwkset.json
mp.jwt.verify.publickey.format=JWKSET
```

The value of the `mp.jwt.verify.publickey.location` property must be a path to the JWK Set file. The file can be located in the application's resources. The following is an example of a JWK Set:

```
{
"kty":"RSA",
"key":"-----BEGIN PUBLIC KEY-----
MIICIjANBgkqhkiG9w0BAQEFAAOCAg8AMIICCgKCAgEAuYP6FyP/cTmVnxE1JXs+5ySE+FNxztk
0aDV8pPiwoZmxIkcH2QYP1XCfY16/mO5zt6nEJbDP7OiWl57bFmuGKTPvf0HXlh17UfStys...
-----END PUBLIC KEY-----",
"e":"AQAB",
"d":"https://www.example.com/key-store.jks"
}
```

Note that the JWT must be signed using the algorithm specified in the header, and the key used to sign the JWT must be in the specified format.

JSON Web Key Set (JWKS)

The JWK Set must contain a single key and the algorithm must be specified in the header of the JWT.

A JWK Set is a JSON data structure representing a set of JWKs. The JWK Set must contain a single key, and the algorithm must be specified in the header of the JWT.

This example shows a JWKS:

```
{
"keys":[
{"kty":"RSA",
```

```
"key":"-----BEGIN PUBLIC KEY-----
MIICIjANBgkqhkiG9w0BAQEFAAOCAg8AMIICCgKCAgEAuYP6FyP/cTmVnxE1JXs+5ySE+FNxztk
OaDV8pPiwoZmxIkcH2QYP1XCfY16/mO5zt6nEJbDP7OiWl57bFmuGKTPvfOHX1h17UfStys...
-----END PUBLIC KEY-----",
"e":"AQAB",
"d":"https://www.example.com/key-store.jks"}]
}
```

To configure a JWK Set, specify the following in your MicroProfile Config:

```
mp.jwt.verify.publickey.location=https://www.example.com/jwkset.json
```

The public key will be read from the URL.

The Jakarta EE Security Specification

The Jakarta EE Security specification defines various mechanisms to secure web services. It can configure basic authentication mechanisms like HTTP Basic and Digest Authentication. It also supports form authentication for web services.

In addition, it provides various options to configure SSL for RESTful web services. If you are using SSL or TLS, the web service client must have a valid certificate to establish a secure connection with the server. Once a connection is established, all data exchanged between the client and server will be encrypted.

Securing a Servlet Using Jakarta Security

The Jakarta Security specifications provide a complete security solution for server-side Java applications. They offer both authentication and authorization services. Authentication is verifying that a user is who they claim to be. Authorization is the process of determining what a user is allowed to do.

The Jakarta Security project offers various mechanisms for securing servlets, including custom authentication.

Form-based authentication is the most common way of authenticating users on the web. In this method, the user is presented with a login form where they enter a username and password. If the credentials are valid, the user is granted access to the protected resources.

Basic authentication is a simpler method of securing servlets. In HTTP basic authentication, the web server prompts the user for a username and password. The credentials are then verified by the server. If the credentials are valid, the user is granted access to the protected resources. HTTP basic authentication transmits the username and password in clear text, which is not as secure as form-based authentication. However, it is possible to use HTTPS with HTTP basic authentication to protect the credentials from being intercepted by attackers.

Digest authentication is like basic authentication, except that the password is not sent in clear text. Instead, a one-way hash of the password is calculated and sent to the server. The server then calculates the hash of the password received and compares it with the sent hash. If they match, then the user is considered authenticated.

Custom authentication allows you to write your authentication code. This is the most flexible way of securing servlets. With custom authentication, you can use any authentication scheme you want.

Both form-based authentication and basic authentication can be used to secure servlets. However, form-based authentication is generally more secure than HTTP Basic authentication. Form-based authentication can also use HTTPS to secure communication between the client and the server. When using HTTPS, the user's credentials are encrypted and cannot be intercepted by third-party attackers.

Jakarta Security also provides a security filter that can be used to secure servlets. The security filter intercepts all requests to the protected resources and verifies that the user has the necessary permissions to access the resources.

To use HTTP basic authentication with a RESTful web service, you need to configure it in the `web.xml` file. The following is the configuration for HTTP basic authentication in the `web.xml` file:

```xml
<security-constraint>
    <web-resource-collection>
        <web-resource-name>secured</web-resource-name>
        <url-pattern>/*</url-pattern>
    </web-resource-collection>
    <auth-constraint>
        <role-name>user</role-name>
    </auth-constraint>
</security-constraint>
```

```
<login-config>
    <auth-method>BASIC</auth-method>
    <realm-name>default</realm-name>
</login-config>
```

This configuration defines a security constraint that restricts access to any resource in the web application to users with the user role. It also configures the web application to use HTTP basic authentication.

Once you have configured HTTP basic authentication, you can access the secured resources using a browser by providing the username and password when prompted. You can also access the secured resource using a tool like curl:

```
curl -u user:password http://localhost:8080/secured
```

This command invokes the "secured" resource on localhost port 8080 with the username and password as user:password.

```
public class SecuredServlet extends HttpServlet {
    @Override
    protected void doGet(HttpServletRequest req, HttpServletResponse
    resp) throws ServletException, IOException {
        // do something
    }
}
```

To test this configuration, you can use curl as follows:

```
$ curl -v http://localhost:8080/secured
```

The server will respond with a 401 unauthorized status code and a WWW-Authenticate header as follows:

```
HTTP/1.1 401 Unauthorized
WWW-Authenticate: Basic realm="default"
```

The client can then resend the request with the appropriate credentials in the Authorization header as follows:

```
$ curl -v -u user:password http://localhost:8080/secured
```

The server will then respond with the resource that was requested:

```
HTTP/1.1 200 OK
Content-Type: text/plain
This is a secured resource.
```

To secure a servlet using Jakarta Security, you need to add the following lines of code to your web.xml file:

```
<security-constraint>
      <web-resource-collection>
            <web-resource-name>secured</web-resource-name>
            <url-pattern>/*</url-pattern>
      </web-resource-collection>
      <auth-constraint>
            <role-name>admin</role-name>
      </auth-constraint>
</security-constraint>

<login-config>
      <auth-method>FORM</auth-method>
      <form-login-config>
            <form-login-page>/login.jsp</form-login-page>
            <form-error-page>/error.jsp</form-error-page>
      </form-login-config>
</login-config>

<security-role>
            <role-name>admin</role-name>
</security-role>
```

In this code, the <security-constraint> element defines a security constraint that applies to all resources in the web application. The <auth-constraint> element specifies that only users with the admin role can access the protected resources. The <login-config> element specifies that form-based authentication will be used. The <form-login-config> element specifies the login page and error page used by the form-based authentication process. Finally, the <security-role> element defines the admin role.

To use digest authentication with a RESTful web service, you need to configure it in the web.xml file.

The following is the configuration for digest authentication in the web.xml file:

```
// ...
<login-config>
<auth-method>DIGEST</auth-method>
<realm-name>default</realm-name>
</login-config>
```

The MicroProfile REST Client

The MicroProfile REST Client is a specification that defines a set of APIs and annotations for building REST clients. It provides a type-safe way to invoke RESTful services. This section shows you how to build a simple MicroProfile REST Client and use it to access a remote service. It also demonstrates how to use the client API to invoke different HTTP methods, such as GET, POST, PUT, and DELETE.

The MicroProfile REST Client is an Eclipse project that provides a portable RESTful client API for Java applications. To view more details about this project, refer to https://github.com/eclipse/microprofile-rest-client. The project is designed to make it easy to write portable and reusable code that can access RESTful services, regardless of the underlying technology or platform.

Add the following dependency to your pom.xml file if you are using Maven to build your application. The MicroProfile REST Client is included in the MicroProfile dependency. To learn more about the MicroProfile project, refer to their official website at https://microprofile.io/.

```
<dependency>
<groupId>org.eclipse.microprofile</groupId>
<artifactId>microprofile</artifactId>
<version>5.0</version>
<type>pom</type>
<scope>provided</scope>
</dependency>
```

Or you can use the REST client dependency specifically, as shown here:

```
<dependency>
<groupId>org.eclipse.microprofile.rest-client</groupId>
<artifactId>microprofile-rest-client-api</artifactId>
<version>1.4</version>
<scope>provided</scope>
</dependency>
```

Here is the server.xml configuration to enable the REST client feature in Open Liberty:

```
<featureManager>
<feature>mpRestClient-3.0</feature>
</featureManager>
```

The @RegisterClient Annotation

The first step is to annotate your client interface with the @RegisterRestClient
annotation. This annotation registers the client with the MicroProfile REST Client
service. The value attribute of this annotation specifies the base URI of the target service:

```
@RegisterRestClient
        (configKey = "systemClient"
         baseUri="http://localhost:9080/api/products")
public interface ProductsClient implements Autoclosable{

        // methods go here
}
```

Configuring Your REST Client

To configure the URI using MicroProfile Config, you need to add a config file named src/
main/webapp/META-INF/microprofile-config.properties to your project. This file
contains the configuration key and value pairs. This example configures the base URI
to http://localhost:8080/api/products. You can also use the Config file to configure
other client properties, such as followRedirects and connectTimeout:

```
systemClient/mp-rest/uri=http://localhost:9080/system
```

REST Client Interface

Here is an example of the REST client interface:

```
@RegisterRestClient
        (configKey = "systemClient"
         baseUri="http://localhost:9080/api/products")
@RegisterProvider(UnknownUriExceptionMapper.class)
@Path("/products")
@Produces("application/json")
@Consumes("application/json")
public interface ProductsClient implements AutoClosable{

    @GET
    List<User> getProducts();

    @GET
    @Path("/{productId}")
    Product getProduct(@PathParam("productId") String productId);

    @POST
    Response createProduct(@HeaderParam("Authorization") String
    authorization,
    Product product);

    @PUT
    @Path("/{productId}")
    Response updateProduct(@BeanParam PutProduct putProduct, Product
    product);

    @DELETE
    @Path("/{productId}")
    Response deleteProduct(@CookieParam("AuthToken") String
    authorization,
    @PathParam("productId") String productId);
}
```

```
public class PutProduct {

        @HeaderParam("Authorization")
        private String authorization;

        @PathParam("productId")
        private String productId;

        // getters, setters, constructors omitted
}
```

The @RegisterProvider annotation registers the ExceptionMapper with the RESTful web services client. It maps the exceptions thrown by a web service client to an HTTP status code. The UnknownUriExceptionMapper class maps the jakarata.ws.rs. NotFoundException exception to a 404 Not Found error.

The ProductsClient interface is annotated with the @jakarta.ws.rs.Path annotation to define the REST endpoints. The @Path annotation specifies a relative path for this resource. The methods in this interface represent the operations that can be performed on the product's resource, such as getting a list of products or getting a specific product.

You can specify the media (MIME) type of the outbound request using the @Consumes annotation. This determines the value of the Content-Type header of the request.

You can also specify the media type of the inbound response using the @Produces annotation, which determines the value of the Accept header of the request.

By default the media types jakarta.ws.rs.core.MediaType.APPLICATION_JSON ("application/json") is used. The REST client will automatically serialize values to JSON unless you explicitly set the media type to something else, such as XML.

If you want to read and write binary data, you can use the byte[] type:

```
// ...
@POST
Response upload(byte[] data);

@GET
byte[] download();
}
```

You can specify path parameters on methods using the @PathParam annotation. For example, this method retrieves a product with a given ID:

```
// ...
@GET
Product getProduct(@PathParam("productId") String productId);
```

The GetProduct method gets a product. It takes the product ID as a path parameter.

The createProduct method creates a new product. It takes in two things: the authorization string and the product itself. The @HeaderParam("Authorization") annotation tells the REST client that the authorization string should be retrieved from the HTTP header. The product is passed in as a POJO object, and it will be converted to a JSON string before being sent to the server.

The deleteProduct method deletes an existing product from the database. It takes in two things: an AuthToken cookie, which is used for authentication, and the ID of product.

The updateProduct method updates an existing product. It takes the PutProduct object, which contains the product ID and authorization string, and the Product object, which contains the updated product information.

The @RestClient annotation is used to mark a field or method as a MicroProfile REST client. Injecting a REST client is similar to injecting any other CDI bean, for example:

```
import org.eclipse.microprofile.rest.client.inject.RestClient;
import jakarta.inject.Inject;
import jakarta.ws.rs.GET;
import jakarta.ws.rs.Path;
import jakarta.ws.rs.PathParam;

public class GreetingService {

    private final GreetingClient greetingClient;

    public GreetingService() {

        // constructor injection
        this.greetingClient = RestClientBuilder.newBuilder()
        .baseUri("http://localhost:8080")
        .build(GreetingClient.class);
    }
```

```
    public String getGreeting() {
        return greetingClient.getGreeting();
    }
}

interface GreetingClient {

    @GET
    @Path("/greeting/{name}")
    String getGreeting(@PathParam("name") String name);
}
```

In this example, the GreetingClient interface is annotated with the @RestClient annotation and is used to invoke a remote REST service.

The GreetingService class injects an instance of the GreetingClient and uses it to invoke the remote REST service.

The RestClientBuilder can be used to configure the injected REST client. In this example, the base URI of the REST service is configured. Other options that can be configured include:

- Registering providers, for example to support JSON-B or Jackson

- Configuring timeouts

- Configuring SSL

- Configuring proxies

For more information, see the MicroProfile REST Client documentation.

The MicroProfile REST Client specification defines a Java API for invoking RESTful services. The API is similar to the JAX-RS 2.0 Client API, but it offers some additional features that are specific to MicroProfile.

The main benefit of the MicroProfile REST Client is that it allows you to invoke REST services without having to write boilerplate code. This can make your code more concise and easier to read.

Another benefit is that the MicroProfile REST Client defines a portable way to configure how the client is created and how it invokes the REST service. This means that you can deploy your application on any MicroProfile runtime and it will work with any compliant REST client implementation.

Documenting RESTful APIs Using MicroProfile OpenAPI

In this section, you learn how to use the MicroProfile OpenAPI annotation to document a REST API. You also learn how to use the OpenAPI UI to view the documentation.

What Is the OpenAPI Specification?

The OpenAPI specification (OAS) defines a standard, language-agnostic interface to RESTful APIs. This makes it easy for third-party tools to generate documentation, client libraries, and other tooling based on the OAS. It was formerly known as Swagger.

The OpenAPI specification is maintained by the OpenAPI Initiative, which is a consortium of industry experts who are committed to standardizing how REST APIs are described.

What Is MicroProfile OpenAPI?

The MicroProfile OpenAPI initiative aims to bring the benefits of the OpenAPI specification to microservices built using the MicroProfile platform. It is a specification that builds on top of the OpenAPI specification and adds capabilities specific to the MicroProfile initiative.

MicroProfile OpenAPI provides tools and APIs that can be used to generate documentation for RESTful APIs. This documentation can be used by developers to understand the API and generate client code. The MicroProfile OpenAPI specification defines a standard format for documenting RESTful APIs.

Using the MicroProfile OpenAPI to Document a REST API

To document a JAX-RS REST API using the MicroProfile OpenAPI, you need to annotate the JAX-RS resource classes and methods with the OpenAPI annotation. The OpenAPI annotation is used to configure the documentation for a JAX-RS resource.

First, you need to add the MicroProfile OpenAPI dependency to your project:

```
<dependency>
<groupId>org.eclipse.microprofile.openapi</groupId>
<artifactId>microprofile-openapi-api</artifactId>
<version>1.0.0</version>
</dependency>
```

Next, you need to configure the OpenAPI documentation. This can be done by using
the @OpenAPIDefinition annotation:

```
import jakarta.ws.rs.GET;
import jakarta.ws.rs.Path;
import org.eclipse.microprofile.openapi.annotations.Operation;
import org.eclipse.microprofile.openapi.annotations.tags.Tag;

import org.eclipse.microprofile.openapi.annotations.OpenAPIDefinition;
import org.eclipse.microprofile.openapi.annotations.info.Info;
import org.eclipse.microprofile.openapi.annotations.servers.Server;

@OpenAPIDefinition(
        info = @Info(
                title = "Products API",
                version = "1.0.0",
                description = "This is Products API."
        ),
        servers = {
                @Server(url = "/api")
        }
)

@Path("/greeting")
public class GreetingResource {

    @GET
    @Operation(summary = "Say hello", tags = {"greeting"})
    public String sayHello() {
            return "Hello";
    }
}
```

The @OpenAPIDefinition annotation configures the overall documentation for
the API. The @Info annotation configures information about the API, such as the title,
version, and description. The @Server annotation configures the URL of the API server.

This example annotates the sayHello() method with the @Operation annotation. This annotation configures information about the operation, such as the summary and tags. The tags can be used to group related operations.

The MicroProfile OpenAPI implementation will generate the documentation for the API based on the annotations. The generated documentation will be in the OpenAPI format.

Table 8-1 lists the commonly used annotations provided by the MicroProfile OpenAPI specification.

Table 8-1. *Annotations in the MicroProfile OpenAPI Specification*

Annotation	Description
@OpenAPIDefinition	Specifies general information about the API, such as the title, version, etc.
@Operation	Specifies information about a single API operation, such as the summary, tags, etc.
@Schema	Specifies information about the data type of a property.
@ParameterIn	Specifies the location of a request parameter, such as QUERY, PATH, etc.
@Callback	Specifies a callback URL for an asynchronous operation.
@Callbacks	Specifies multiple @Callback annotations.

Viewing the Generated Documentation

To view the generated documentation, you can use the OpenAPI UI tool. OpenAPI UI is a web-based tool that can be used to view the documentation for a REST API.

The OpenAPI UI tool can be accessed at the following URL:

```
http://localhost:8080/openapi/
```

The /openapi endpoint gets information about the OpenAPI specification generated from the comments in the source code annotations. It returns information in YAML format.

Summary

In this chapter, you learned how to use the MicroProfile JWT Auth specification to validate the signature of a JWT. You also learned how to configure your application to use a JWK Set or a PEM-encoded public key. In the next chapter, you learn about containerizing your applications using Docker and Kubernetes to manage deployment.

CHAPTER 9

Containerizing Microservices Using Kubernetes

This chapter explains how to containerize your microservices using Docker and Kubernetes. You will start by learning about containers and why you should use them. You'll then learn how to install Docker and Kubernetes. Finally, you will learn how to deploy your microservices into containers using Docker and Kubernetes.

What Are Containers?

Containers are a way to package software so that it can run isolated from other software on the same host. This is different from virtualization, where each guest operating system has its kernel and runs in its isolated environment.

Containerizing a microservice is a great way to improve the overall reliability and resilience of your system. Containers allow you to package your microservice with all its dependencies into a single unit. This makes it easy to deploy and manage your microservices.

Why Use Containers?

There are many reasons to use containers, but the main reasons are as follows:

© Tarun Telang 2023
T. Telang, *Beginning Cloud Native Development with MicroProfile, Jakarta EE, and Kubernetes*,
https://doi.org/10.1007/978-1-4842-8832-0_9

- **Portability:** Containers can be easily moved from one host to another. This is because they do not depend on the host operating system.

- **Isolation:** Containers are isolated from each other and the host operating system. If one container crashes, it will not affect the other containers.

- **Efficiency:** Containers use fewer resources than virtual machines. This is because each container shares the host operating system kernel.

What Is Container Orchestration?

Container orchestration is the process of automating the deployment, management, and scaling of containerized applications. The most popular container orchestration tool is Kubernetes.

Kubernetes is an open-source system for automating the deployment, scaling, and management of containerized applications. It was initially designed by Google and is now maintained by the Cloud Native Computing Foundation. Kubernetes is a portable, extensible, open-source platform for managing containerized workloads and services that facilitates declarative configuration and automation. It has a large, rapidly growing ecosystem. Kubernetes services, support, and tools are widely available.

The Benefits of Using Container Orchestration

There are many benefits of using container orchestration, but these are the main benefits:

- **Improved efficiency:** Container orchestration tools can improve the efficiency of your workflow by automating many of the tasks required to manage many containers.

- **Increased flexibility:** Container orchestration tools can make deploying and managing applications in various environments easier.

- **Improved scalability:** Container orchestration tools can improve the scalability of your application by making it easy to add or remove containers as needed.

- **Increased security:** Containers are isolated from each other and the host operating system, making it difficult for malicious actors to access your data or infect your systems.

- **Reduced costs:** Containers can help you reduce the cost of running your applications by using fewer resources.

- **Easier debugging:** Container orchestration tools make it easier to debug problems with your application by providing a single view into all the containers in your system.

Understanding Kubernetes Terminology

Before you dive deeper and start using Kubernetes to manage your containers, you should familiarize yourself with some of the important terminology related to Kubernetes.

Pod: A group of one or more containers with shared storage/network and a specification for how to run the containers. A pod represents a unit of deployment; a single application container, or set of collocated containers, that you want to run as a group on a Kubernetes node.

Kubelet: A kubelet is a process that runs on each worker node and manages pods on the node. The kubelet ensures that the pods are running and healthy. It also communicates with the master nodes to coordinate the deployment of applications on the nodes.

Node: A worker machine in Kubernetes; part of a cluster. Depending on the cluster, a node can be a VM or a physical machine (bare-metal). Each node runs Kubernetes agents and is managed by the master components.

Worker node: Runs your applications and cloud services. Worker nodes host pods and run the containers in those pods. Each worker node has a kubelet and a kube-proxy running on it.

- The *kubelet* is responsible for running and managing pods on the node.

- A *kube-proxy* is a process that runs on each worker node and manages networking for the services on the node. It is responsible for networking and load balancing for the services on the node. The kube-proxy ensures that traffic to the services is appropriately routed.

Control plane node: Runs the Kubernetes control plane components, including the API server, scheduler, and controller manager. There is only one control plane node in a cluster. You do not run user-provided applications on a control plane node.

Master node: The node that runs the Kubernetes master components. A Kubernetes cluster has only one master node. A master node is used to manage the Kubernetes cluster. The master node has several processes running on it, including the kube-apiserver, kube-controller-manager, and kube-scheduler.

- The *kube-apiserver* exposes the Kubernetes API. The kubelet uses it to communicate with the master node.

- The *kube-controller-manager* manages replication controllers and services. It is responsible for ensuring that the desired state is maintained for the applications running in the cluster.

- The *kube-scheduler* schedules pods to run on nodes. It is responsible for ensuring that the applications are balanced across the nodes in the cluster.

Kubernetes cluster: A set of machines, called nodes, that run containerized applications.

Service: A pod that is exposed to the network to serve traffic. Kubernetes creates a corresponding load balancer to route traffic to your pod when you create a service.

Replication controller: A replication controller ensures that a specified number of pod replicas are running at any given time. If there are too few replicas, the controller creates more. If there are too many replicas, the controller deletes extras. A typical use case for a replication controller is to ensure that a specified number of web servers are running at all times.

Labels: Key/value pairs attached to objects, such as pods. Labels enable users to organize and select groups of objects.

Annotations: Key/value pairs attached to objects, such as pods. Annotations do not affect the identity of an object, but they can be used to store arbitrary data for documentation or other purposes.

The Key Features of Kubernetes

Kubernetes is a popular choice for deploying containerized applications today. It offers many features, such as:

- **Automatic deployment:** Kubernetes can automatically deploy your applications when there are changes to the codebase and can roll back deployments if necessary.

- **Storage orchestration:** Kubernetes can automatically provision storage for applications and support various storage backends. It can automatically mount storage systems, such as local storage, public cloud providers, and more.

- **Rolling updates:** Kubernetes can perform rolling updates of applications, which means it can update an application one node at a time without disrupting service. It rolls out new versions of an application while ensuring no downtime.

- **Automatic bin-packing:** Kubernetes automatically schedules containers onto cluster nodes to efficiently use available resources.

- **Monitoring:** Kubernetes can generate detailed logs and monitoring data for all aspects of the system, which can be used to troubleshoot problems or optimize performance.

- **Health checks:** Kubernetes can perform health checks on applications to ensure that they are running as expected, and it can restart or replace unhealthy components if necessary.

- **Self-healing:** If a node fails in a Kubernetes cluster, the system will detect the failure and schedule the affected pods to run on other nodes.

- **Horizontal scaling:** Kubernetes makes it easy to scale your application by adding or removing nodes in the cluster as needed.

- **Auto-scaling:** Kubernetes can automatically scale applications up or down based on traffic levels and can also scale individual components of an application separately.

- **Distribution of the load:** Kubernetes can distribute the load between different nodes in a cluster and automatically schedule applications to run on specific nodes based on available resources.

- **Service discovery and load balancing:** Kubernetes automatically assigns a unique IP address to each pod in the cluster and can load-balance traffic across them.

- **Secrets and configuration management**: Using secrets, Kubernetes can store and manage sensitive information, such as passwords and API keys. Configuration data can be stored in config maps.

Using Kubernetes

Kubernetes can be used to manage containerized applications at scale in a variety of ways. The most common way is to use a managed Kubernetes service from a public cloud provider, such as Google Kubernetes Engine (GKE) or Amazon Elastic Container Service for Kubernetes (EKS). These services take care of all the infrastructure management tasks, such as provisioning nodes, deploying Kubernetes, and more.

Another option is installing and managing Kubernetes using tools such as *kubeadm*. This can be a good choice if you want more control over the infrastructure or if you're running Kubernetes in a private data center.

Kubernetes can also be used to manage non-containerized applications. This is done by creating so-called "bare-metal" clusters, which can be used to deploy and manage VMs or even physical servers.

Once Kubernetes is up and running, you can use it to deploy applications using a variety of methods. The most common way is to use container images, which can be pulled from a public registry such as Docker Hub or a private registry. You can also use Kubernetes to deploy source code directly, using a build tool such as Jenkins.

Kubernetes is also often used with other tools, such as Prometheus (`https://prometheus.io/`) for monitoring, Istio (`https://istio.io/`) for service mesh, and Helm (`https://helm.sh/`) for package management.

Using Docker Containers

First, make sure you have Docker installed on your system. To containerize an application, you need to create a Dockerfile. A Dockerfile is a text file that contains the commands used to build and run your container. In the Dockerfile, you specify the base image you want to use for your container and the commands that will be used to build and run your application.

A base image is a pre-built image that can be used to create new images. For example, if you wanted to create an image for an Open Liberty Server, you could use a base image with Java runtime and an Open Liberty server installed and configured. This would save you from having to install Open Liberty in your image. There are many different base images available, and you can even create your own. To find a base image that suits your needs, you can search through the Docker Hub repository. Once you have selected a base image, you must create a Dockerfile.

The contents of the Dockerfile are as follows:

```
FROM open-liberty

ARG VERSION=1.0
ARG REVISION=SNAPSHOT

LABEL \
org.opencontainers.image.authors="Tarun Telang" \  name="demo"  \
version="$VERSION-$REVISION" \
summary="A sample microservice."    \
description="An image containing a sample microservice running with the
Open Liberty runtime." \

COPY --chown=1001:0 src/main/liberty/config/ /config/
COPY --chown=1001:0 target/*.war /config/apps/

RUN configure.sh
```

The first line in the file specifies the base image to use. This example uses the openliberty/open-liberty base image. The second line copies the configuration files for the application into the /config directory in the container. The third line copies the WAR file for the application into the /config/apps directory. The final line runs the configure.sh script, which will apply the configuration files to the server.

Running a MicroProfile Application in Docker

As a first step, run the following command in your project directory so that a .war file is built in your project's target directory.

```
$ mvn package
```

The mvn package command builds a .war file. The generated .war file can be found in the target directory.

When the project has been successfully built, you should see the following output:

```
...
...
[INFO] Building war: /home/project/mp-demo/target/product-ws.war
[INFO] ------------------------------------------------------------------------
[INFO] BUILD SUCCESS
[INFO] ------------------------------------------------------------------------
[INFO] Total time:  7.826 s
[INFO] Finished at: 2022-08-28T20:53:07Z
[INFO] ------------------------------------------------------------------------
```

Next, run the following command to download the latest Open Liberty Docker image:

```
$ docker pull open-liberty
```

The docker pull command will pull the latest Open Liberty image from the Docker Hub. You will see the following output once the Docker image for Open Liberty has been successfully downloaded.

```
Using default tag: latest
latest: Pulling from library/open-liberty
0c673eb68f88: Already exists
028bdc977650: Already exists
1ccd5c23a917: Pull complete
8619a97d585d: Pull complete
939335e1685d: Pull complete
38d0c214fbd9: Pull complete
```

```
2e17378e4efe: Pull complete
79d116412958: Pull complete
cf67e7591f9b: Pull complete
bb086ba294ec: Pull complete
ee1c870013e1: Pull complete
Digest: sha256:fcc5e656cfcd08ca308214c4163e0eae4c8d3016af4e3fc43a95ff
ea96800d72
Status: Downloaded newer image for openliberty/open-liberty:latest
docker.io/openliberty/open-liberty:latest
```

Now, as you have the base image downloaded, you can build an image using the docker build command:

```
$ docker build -t openliberty-mp-demo:1.0-SNAPSHOT .
```

This will create an image called openliberty-mp-demo using the contents of the Dockerfile. Upon successful completion of this command, you'll see this output:

```
Sending build context to Docker daemon     146MB
Step 1/7 : FROM openliberty/open-liberty
 ---> b5cd482cfb55
Step 2/7: ARG VERSION=1.0
 ---> Running in 9cbbafc3e3c1
Removing intermediate container 9cbbafc3e3c1
 ---> 88df52795daf
Step 3/7 : ARG REVISION=SNAPSHOT
 ---> Running in 0b521ef54703
Removing intermediate container 0b521ef54703
 ---> ae93b14e7aa0
Step 4/7 : LABEL    org.opencontainers.image.authors="Tarun
Telang"   name="demo"   version="$VERSION-$REVISION"   summary="The sample
microservice"   description="This image contains the a sample microservice
running with the Open Liberty runtime."
 ---> Running in bbe0c0484328
Removing intermediate container bbe0c0484328
 ---> e48ec9d295d9
```

```
Step 5/7 : COPY --chown=1001:0 src/main/liberty/config/ /config/
 ---> 241c3e8f4355
Step 6/7 : COPY --chown=1001:0 target/*.war /config/apps/
 ---> 2b16449cf495
Step 7/7 : RUN configure.sh
 ---> Running in fa6715060554
Removing intermediate container fa6715060554
 ---> af7f2ca5b7cd
Successfully built af7f2ca5b7cd
Successfully tagged openliberty-getting-started:1.0-SNAPSHOT
```

To verify that the image is built, run the docker images command to list all local Docker images:

```
$ docker images
```

You should see a row containing your Docker image in the list of Docker images, as shown here:

```
REPOSITORY            TAG             IMAGE ID        CREATED       SIZE
openliberty-mp-demo   1.0-SNAPSHOT    b5cd482cfb55    3 weeks ago   886MB
```

You can now run your application by using the docker run command:

```
$ docker run -d --name product-ws -p 9080:9080 openliberty-mp-
demo:1.0-SNAPSHOT
```

This will start a Docker container with the name product-ws. The -d option is used to run the container in *detached* mode. The -p option maps the ports between the host and the container. In this case, port 9080 inside the container will be mapped to the same ports on your local machine.

You can verify if the container is running by using the docker ps command, as shown here:

```
$ docker ps
```

Ensure the status of the container is up.

This will start a container using the my-liberty-app image and map port 9080 on the host machine to port 9080 in the container. You should now be able to access your application at `http://localhost:9080`. The application will be accessible at the same URL even if you are running it inside a Docker container.

You can stop the application by using the following command:

```
$ docker stop product-ws
```

The `docker stop` command is used to stop a running container. In this example, you stop the container with the name `product-ws`.

To remove the container, run the following command:

```
$ docker rm product-ws
```

The `docker rm` command is used to remove a stopped container. In this example, you remove the container with the name `product-ws`.

To remove the image, run the following command:

```
$ docker rmi openliberty/open-liberty
```

The `docker rmi` command is used to remove an image. In this example, you remove the image with the name `openliberty/open-liberty`.

Pushing the Docker Image to Docker Hub

If you don't have a Docker Hub account, create one first. Once you have a Docker Hub account, log in to it using the following command:

```
$ docker login -u <username> -p <password>
```

Replace `<username>` and `<password>` with your Docker Hub username and password.

```
WARNING! Using --password via the CLI is insecure. Use --password-stdin.
WARNING! Your password will be stored unencrypted in /home/theia/.docker/
config.json.
Configure a credential helper to remove this warning. See
https://docs.docker.com/engine/reference/commandline/
login/#credentials-store

Login Succeeded
```

If you see this output, you are successfully logged in to Docker Hub. You must tag your image before you can push it to Docker Hub. The Docker Hub uses these tags as namespaces to identify the images.

To tag your image, run the following command:

```
docker tag <image-id> <username>/< image-name >:<tag>
```

For example, if your username is taruntelang and your repository is openliberty-mp-demo, you would tag your image like this:

```
$ docker tag openliberty-mp-demo:1.0-SNAPSHOT taruntelang/openliberty-mp-demo:1.0-SNAPSHOT
```

The latest tag indicates that this is the most recent version of the image. You can also use other tags, such as v1 or 2.0, to indicate different versions of your image.

To push the image to Docker Hub, run the following command:

```
$ docker push <username>/<image-name>:<tag>
```

Replace <username> with your Docker Hub username, <imagename> with the name of your image, and <tag> with a tag for the image. For example, you can use 1.0-SNAPSHOT as the tag. In this case, you would run the following command:

```
$ docker push taruntelang/openliberty-mp-demo:1.0-SNAPSHOT
```

You can verify that your image is published by visiting hub.docker.com. After signing into your Docker Hub account, you should see the image in Figure 9-1.

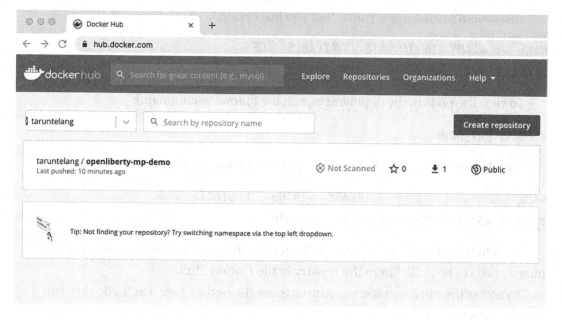

Figure 9-1. *Docker images in the Docker registry of your Docker Hub account*

Now that the Docker Image is available on Docker Hub, you can deploy it to Kubernetes.

To deploy the Docker image to Kubernetes, run the following command:

```
kubectl create deployment <deploymentname> --image=<username>/<imagenam
e>:<tag>
```

Replace <deploymentname> with a name for the deployment, <username> with your Docker Hub username, <imagename> with the name of your image, and <tag> with the tag for the image.

In this case, you need to run the following command:

```
$ kubectl create deployment mp-demo --image=taruntelang/openliberty-mp-
demo:1.0-SNAPSHOT
```

This will create a deployment in Kubernetes and result in the following output.

```
deployment.apps/mp-demo created
```

To view the deployment, run the following command:

```
$ kubectl get deployments
```

You should see the deployment that you just created.

```
NAME      READY  UP-TO-DATE  AVAILABLE  AGE
mp-demo   0/1    1           0          2m7s
```

To view the pods in the deployment, run the following command:

```
kubectl get pods
```

You should see the pod that is running your microservice:

```
NAME                        READY  STATUS   RESTARTS  AGE
mp-demo-65fc677585-mdzrg    1/1    Running  0         2m46s
```

It could take some time for your deployments and pods to be ready, as the Docker image needs to be pulled from the registry in the Docker Hub.

To access the microservice, you must expose the pod as a service. To do this, run the following command:

```
$ kubectl expose deployment <deployment-name> --type=LoadBalancer
--port=<port>
```

Replace <deployment-name> with the deployment name and <port> with the port on which the microservice is running. For example, if the microservice runs on port 9080, you would use 9080 as the value for <port>.

```
$ kubectl expose deployment mp-demo --type=LoadBalancer --port=9080
service/mp-demo exposed
```

This will create a service in Kubernetes. To view the service, run the following command:

```
kubectl get services
```

You should see the service that you just created.

```
NAME      TYPE          CLUSTER-IP     EXTERNAL-IP
PORT(S)              AGE
mp-demo   LoadBalancer  172.21.121.32  69fd7a23-us-east.lb.appdomain.cloud
9080:30390/TCP       59s
```

You can use these details to access the microservice.

Congratulations! You have successfully deployed a microservice to Kubernetes.

Scaling Your Deployment

Kubernetes makes it easy to scale deployments. To scale a deployment, run the following command:

```
kubectl scale deployment <deploymentname> --replicas=<numberofreplicas>
```

Replace <deploymentname> with the deployment name and <numberofreplicas> with the number of replicas. For example, to scale the deployment to four replicas, you would use --replicas=4.

```
$ kubectl scale deployment ms-deployment --replicas=4
deployment.extensions/mp-deployment scaled
```

To view the deployment, run the following command:

```
$ kubectl get deployments
```

You should see that the deployment has been scaled to four replicas.

```
NAME            READY  UP-TO-DATE  AVAILABLE  AGE
mp-deployment   4/4    4           4          4m38s
```

To view the pods in the deployment, run the following command:

```
kubectl get pods
```

You should see that there are four pods now.

```
NAME                                READY  STATUS   RESTARTS  AGE
mp-demo-7d4c44f8-7bb9c5b68b-6tgxq   1/1    Running  0         4m38s
mp-demo-7d4c44f8-7bb9c5b68b-hg78w   1/1    Running  0         4m38s
mp-demo-7d4c44f8-7bb9c5b68b-1z6n1   1/1    Running  0         4m38s
mp-demo-7d4c44f8-7bb9c5b68b-x6wnf   1/1    Running  0         4m38s
```

You can also use kubectl to delete deployments. To delete a deployment, run the following command:

```
kubectl delete deployment <deploymentname>
```

Replace <deploymentname> with the name of the deployment you want to delete.

```
$ kubectl delete deployment ms-deployment
```

```
deployment.extensions "ms-deployment" deleted
```

You can also use kubectl to delete services. To delete a service, run the following command:

```
$ kubectl delete service <servicename>
```

Replace `<servicename>` with the name of the service you want to delete.

```
$ kubectl delete service ms-service
service "ms-service" deleted
```

You have learned how to containerize a microservice using Docker and deploy it on a Kubernetes cluster.

Summary

In this chapter, you started by learning what containers are and why you should use them. Next, you learned about container orchestration. You also learned about the essential features and terminology of Kubernetes. You learned how to containerize a microservice using Docker and deploy it on a Kubernetes cluster. Finally, you learned how to scale deployments and delete them when needed. Here are the key takeaways from this chapter:

- Containerization is a way to package software so that it can run isolated from other software on the same host, which improves reliability and resilience. Containers package your microservice with all its dependencies into a single unit that is portable, easy to deploy, and easy to manage.

- Container orchestration is the process of automating containerized applications' deployment, management, and scaling. Kubernetes is the most popular container orchestration tool. Container orchestration improves efficiency and security, reduces cost, simplifies debugging, and increases flexibility and scalability of the application running in containers.

Here are some of the essential Kubernetes terms you should remember.

- A *pod* is a group of containers deployed on the same host. Pods provide colocation and communication between containers.

- A *service* is an abstraction that defines a logical set of pods and provides stable networking to those pods. Services enable loose coupling between microservices.

- A *deployment* is an object that describes the desired state for a group of pods. A deployment ensures that the desired state is maintained even if the pods are deleted or restarted.

- A *node* is a worker machine in Kubernetes. Each node has a pod running on it. Nodes communicate with each other using the Kubernetes API.

- A *worker node* is a machine used to run containers. A worker node can be a physical or virtual machine.

- A *master node* is a machine used to manage the Kubernetes cluster.

- A group of nodes is called a *cluster*.

- *Labels* are key/value pairs attached to objects, such as pods. They are used to identify and select groups of objects.

- *Selectors* are used to select a group of objects based on their labels.

- *Annotations* are used to store non-identifying metadata about objects.

Key features of Kubernetes include management, automatic deployment, storage orchestration, rolling updates, automatic bin-packing, monitoring, health checks, horizontal scaling, auto-scaling, load balancing, service discovery, secrets and configuration management, and load distribution of containerized applications.

A Dockerfile is used to create a Docker image. A base image is a starting point for creating a new image. A Docker image is a read-only template that contains a set of instructions to create a container. You can get base images from Docker Hub or other repositories.

You need to write a Dockerfile and run the `docker build` command to build a Docker image.

```
docker login --username=<your-dockerhub-username> --email=<your-email
@company.com>
```

```
docker images
```

```
docker tag <imageid> <your-dockerhub-username>/<repository>:<tag>
```

```
docker push <your-dockerhub-username>/<repository>:<tag>
```

Before deploying the Docker image to Kubernetes, you need to push it to a registry. You can push the image to Docker Hub or other registries such as Google Container Registry (GCR).

Kubectl is a command-line tool used to manage Kubernetes objects. You can use kubectl to create, delete, update, and view Kubernetes objects such as pods, services, and deployments.

In this chapter, you learned how to package your microservice into a Docker image and deploy it on a Kubernetes cluster.

You can use Kubernetes by installing it on your own infrastructure or by using a managed Kubernetes service, such as Google Kubernetes Engine (GKE).

kubectl is the command-line tool that can manage Kubernetes deployments and is used to interact with Kubernetes. Here are the commands you learned.

- `kubectl get`: Get information about Kubernetes resources

- `kubectl describe`: Get detailed information about Kubernetes resources

- `kubectl scale`: Scaling means increasing or decreasing the number of replicas in a deployment. This can be done using this command.

Finally, to delete a deployment, use the `kubectl delete` deployment command. To delete a service, use the `kubectl delete service <service-name>` command.

APPENDIX A

Introduction to Maven

Maven is a build automation tool used primarily for Java projects. In a nutshell, Maven can help you manage a project's build, reporting, and documentation needs from a central piece of information.

Note According to Apache Software Foundation, Apache Maven is a software project management and comprehension tool. Based on the concept of a project object model (POM), it can manage a project's build, reporting, and documentation needs from a central place.

Features of Maven

Maven is a popular build tool for Java projects. It offers several benefits over other build tools, such as Apache ant (`https://ant.apache.org/`). Maven provides a wide range of features, which can be divided into the following categories:

- **Build system:** Maven can be used as a build system for Java projects. It provides a wide range of plugins that can be used to compile, test, and package the code.

- **Dependency management:** Maven can manage dependencies for a project. This includes downloading the dependencies from a repository and adding them to the project's classpath.

- **Documentation:** Maven can generate documentation for a project, which includes API documentation as well as reports on tests, code coverage, and so on.

© Tarun Telang 2023
T. Telang, *Beginning Cloud Native Development with MicroProfile, Jakarta EE, and Kubernetes*,
https://doi.org/10.1007/978-1-4842-8832-0

- **Reporting:** Maven can generate a wide range of reports on the health of a project, such as code quality, test coverage, and so on.

- **Release management:** Maven can be used for release management for a project. This includes tagging versions, creating release notes, and uploading the artifacts to a repository.

Maven Lifecycle

Maven is based on a central concept called the *lifecycle*. The Maven Lifecycle is an ordered set of phases a project goes through during its development. When you build a project, Maven will go through these phases in order, executing each one as it goes. The following are the standard phases in the Maven lifecycle:

- **Validate and process resources:** This phase validates that the project is correct and that all necessary resources for the project are available, such as images, XML files, and so on.

- **Compile:** This phase compiles the source code of the project.

- **Process classes:** This phase post-processes the compiled source code, for example, to add debugging information.

- **Generate test sources:** This phase generates the test source code for the project.

- **Process test resources:** This phase processes the resources of the test source code, such as images, XML files, and so on.

- **Test compile:** This phase compiles the test source code.

- **Test:** This phase tests the compiled source code using a suitable unit testing framework. These tests should not require the code to be packaged or deployed.

- **Prepare package:** This phase prepares the package to be installed, such as creating the manifest file.

- **Package:** This phase packages the compiled source code into a distributable format, such as a JAR.

- **Install:** This phase installs the package into the local repository for use as a dependency in other local projects.

- **Deploy:** This phase copies the final package to the remote repository for sharing with other developers and projects.

Benefits of Maven

There are many benefits of using Maven for your build process:

- **Simplifies the build process:** You no longer have to manage dependencies manually. Maven will automatically download the required dependencies and insert them into your project.

- **Makes it easy to manage dependencies:** Maven uses a standard directory layout and a default build lifecycle. This makes it easy to know where your files are and what the role of each file is.

- **Provides consistent builds:** With Maven, it is easy to maintain your project's build across different environments.

- **Facilitates easier collaboration:** Maven provides good project documentation.

- **Makes it easy to start new projects:** Maven provides a standard directory layout and an easy way to create a new Java project. This makes it easier for new developers to join the project.

- **Supports the principle of convention over configuration:** This means that Maven will automatically apply sensible defaults to your project. You can override these defaults as necessary.

- **Improves team collaboration:** Maven provides an easy way for developers to share information about the project's build. This makes it easier for teams to work together on projects.

- **Facilitates easy integration with IDE:** Maven provides tight integration with popular IDEs such as Eclipse, NetBeans, and IntelliJ IDEA. This makes it easier for developers to work with Maven projects.

- **Quality project information:** Maven generates standard reports about the health of your project, including test reports, code coverage reports, and static code analysis reports. This makes it easy for you to see how your project is doing.

- **Makes it easy to find dependencies:** Maven's central repository contains a huge amount of Java libraries and artifacts. This makes it easy for you to find dependencies.

- **Transparent migration to new features:** Maven offers a consistent way to upgrade project dependencies, plugins, and goals. This makes it easy for you to stay up-to-date with the latest features.

- **Extensibility:** Maven is highly extensible. You can easily add new plugins or customize existing ones.

- **Automates common tasks:** Maven can automatically run tasks, such as compiling source code, generating documentation, and packaging the project. This saves you time and effort.

- **Makes it easy to release projects:** Maven provides a standard way to release projects. This makes it easy for developers to deploy projects.

How Does Maven Benefit the Development Process?

Maven can help improve the development process in many ways:

1. It can help reduce the complexity of the build process, making it more streamlined and easier to understand.

2. It can help manage dependencies more effectively, leading to fewer potential conflicts and less need for manual updates.

3. It can provide consistent builds across different machines and environments, making it easier to ensure that all developers are working with the same codebase.

4. It can improve team collaboration by providing a standard way for developers to share information about the build process.

5. It can facilitate easy integration with IDEs, making it simpler for developers to work with Maven projects.

6. It can generate quality project information, such as code coverage reports and static code analysis reports.

7. It can offer a transparent way to migrate to new features, making it easier to stay up-to-date with the latest developments.

8. It is highly extensible, allowing developers to add new plugins or customize existing ones easily.

The Maven Architecture

Maven is a declarative tool, meaning that it does not require developers to write extensive configuration files. Instead, Maven uses a standard directory layout and a default build lifecycle. This makes it easy for developers to know where their files are and what the role of each file is.

Maven is also highly extensible. Developers can easily add new plugins or customize existing ones to suit their needs.

Maven's architecture is based on three concepts: project object model (POM), plugins, and goals.

- The *POM* is the central element of Maven. It is an XML file that contains information about the project, such as the name, version, dependencies, and build settings.

- *Plugins* are components that extend Maven's functionality. They are used to execute common tasks, such as compiling code or creating a JAR file.

- *Goals* are the specific actions that a plugin executes. For example, the compile goal of the Java compiler plugin will compile the project's code.

Maven's standard directory layout is based on the Filesystem Hierarchy Standard. This layout defines a consistent structure for all Maven projects, making it easy for developers to know where their files are and what the role of each file is.

What Is a Maven Repository?

A Maven *repository* is a directory where all the project JARs, library JARs, plugins, or any other project-specific artifacts are stored and can be used by Maven. There are three types of repositories:

- **Local repository:** This is a directory on the developer's machine, where all the dependencies are stored locally.

- **Central repository:** This is a repository maintained by Apache, which contains most of the common dependencies.

- **Remote repositories:** These are repositories maintained by third parties, which can be used to download dependencies.

Using Maven to Create a Java Project

Creating a Java project with Maven is easy. Simply run the following command from the terminal:

```
$ mvn archetype:generate -DgroupId=com.example -DartifactId=my-project
-DarchetypeArtifactId=maven-archetype-quickstart
-DinteractiveMode=false
```

This will generate a simple Java project with the following structure:

```
my-project
├── pom.xml
├── src
├── main
│   └── java
│       └── com
│           └── example
│               └── App.java
└── test
    └── java
        └── com
            └── example
                └── AppTest.java
```

Using Maven in Your Project

You can use Maven in your project by adding the following lines to your pom.xml file:

```
1   <project>
2   <modelVersion>4.0.0</modelVersion>
3   <groupId>com.example</groupId>
4   <artifactId>my-project</artifactId>
5   <version>1.0-SNAPSHOT</version>
6   <dependencies>
7   <dependency>
8   <groupId>junit</groupId>
9   <artifactId>junit</artifactId>
10  <version>4.12</version>
11  <scope>test</scope>
12  </dependency>
13  </dependencies>
14  <build>
15  <plugins>
16  <plugin>                <         <groupId>org.apache.maven.plugins</groupId>
17  <artifactId>maven-compiler-plugin</artifactId>
18  <version>3.5.1</version>
19  <configuration>
20  <source>1.8</source>
21  <target>1.8</target>
22  </configuration>
23  </plugin>
24  </plugins>
25  </build>
26  </project>
27
```

Explanation:

- Line 1: The <project> element is the root element of the pom.xml file.

- Line 2: The <modelVersion> element indicates the version of the POM model being used.

- Line 3: The `<groupId>` element indicates the group ID of the project.

- Line 4: The `<artifactId>` element indicates the artifact ID of the project.

- Line 5: The `<version>` element indicates the version of the project.

- Line 6: The `<dependencies>` element indicates the project's dependencies.

- Line 7: The `<dependency>` element indicates a single dependency of the project.

- Line 8: The `<groupId>` element indicates the group ID of the dependency.

- Line 9: The `<artifactId>` element indicates the artifact ID of the dependency. The JUnit dependency is used to unit test the project code.

- Line 10: The `<version>` element indicates the version of the dependency.

- Line 11: The `<scope>` element indicates the scope of the dependency. There are five possible scopes for a dependency: `compile`, `runtime`, `test`, `provided`, and `system`. The `compile` scope indicates that the dependency is required at compile time. The `runtime` scope indicates that the dependency is required at runtime. The `test` scope indicates that the dependency is required for tests. The `provided` scope indicates that the dependency is available to the compiler, but not required. The `system` scope indicates that the dependency is required by the system. In this case, the scope is set to `test`, which means that the dependency is only available for testing.

- Line 12: The `</dependency>` element ends the configuration for a single dependency.

- Line 13: The `</dependencies>` element ends the configuration for all dependencies.

- Line 14: The `<build>` element indicates the build configuration for the project.

- Line 15: The `<plugins>` element indicates the build plugins for the project.

- Line 16: The `<plugin>` element indicates a single build plugin.

- Line 17: The `<groupId>` element indicates the group ID of the build plugin.

- Line 18: The `<artifactId>` element indicates the artifact ID of the build plugin. The `maven-compiler-plugin` is used to compile Java source code.

- Line 19: The `<version>` element indicates the version of the build plugin.

- Line 20: The `<configuration>` element indicates the configuration for the build plugin.

- Line 21: The `<source>` element indicates the Java source version.

- Line 22: The `<target>` element indicates the Java target version.

- Line 23: The `</configuration>` element ends the configuration for the build plugin.

- Line 24: The `</plugin>` element ends the configuration for a single build plugin.

- Line 25: The `</plugins>` element ends the configuration for all build plugins.

- Line 26: The `</build>` element ends the build configuration for the project.

- Line 27: The `</project>` element ends the configuration for the POM.

Useful Maven Commands

The following command tells you what the `maven-compiler-plugin` does.

```
mvn help:describe -Dplugin=org.apache.maven.plugins:maven-compiler-plugin
```

The command invokes the `describe` goal of the `help` plugin specified as `help:describe`. The goal takes arguments from the command line, which you specify using -D. The -Dplugin argument specifies the plugin you want to get details for.

What Is the Difference Between a Snapshot and a Release?

A *snapshot* is a version of a project that is under development and may not be stable. A *release* is a version of a project that is considered stable and is ready for production use.

Creating an Open Liberty Project Using Maven

In this appendix, you learn how to create an Open Liberty project using Maven. It walks you through the steps necessary to create a simple project using Open Liberty and Maven.

Creating a new Open Liberty project using Maven is simple. The first step is to generate a basic project structure by using the `maven archetype:generate` command.

An *archetype* is a template for a project. It provides the basic structure and files needed for a particular type of project. This archetype is available at the Maven Central Repository.

The *Maven Central Repository* is a collection of software artifacts that are used by Maven-based projects. It contains artifacts for a wide variety of projects, from the Jakarta EE project to popular open-source projects like Spring and Hibernate.

Generating a Web Project Using Maven

To generate a web project, use the `liberty-archetype-webapp` archetype. Run the following command from the directory where you want your project to be created:

```
$ mvn archetype:generate
-DarchetypeGroupId="io.openliberty.tools"
-DarchetypeArtifactId="liberty-archetype-webapp"
-DarchetypeVersion="3.6.1"
-DgroupId="<com.mycompany.app>"
-DartifactId="<artifactId>"
-DinteractiveMode=false
```

T. Telang, *Beginning Cloud Native Development with MicroProfile, Jakarta EE, and Kubernetes*, https://doi.org/10.1007/978-1-4842-8832-0

Explanation:

- Replace <artifactId> and <groupId> with the artifact name and group ID of your application.

- The archetypeGroupId parameter specifies the group of the archetype to use. This example uses io.openliberty.tools.

- The archetypeArtifactId specifies the artifact within the group that you want to use, which is liberty-plugin-archetype. Finally, specify the version number as 3.6.1.

This command will create a new project. The folder structure of the generated project is as follows:

```
<artifactId>
|    ├── pom.xml
|    └── src
|        └── main
|            ├── java
|            |   └── <My-groupId>
|            |       └── HelloServlet.java
|            ├── liberty
|            |   └── config
|            |       └── server.xml
|            └── webapp
|                └── WEB-INF
|        └── index.html
└── pom.xml
```

This will generate a basic project structure with the following files and directories:

- pom.xml: The Maven project file contains information about the project, such as dependencies, plugins, and goals.

- src/main/java: This directory contains the Java source code for the project.

- src/main/resources: This directory contains resources such as property files and web application assets.

- `src/test/java`: This directory contains JUnit tests.

- `liberty/config/server.xml`: This file contains the configuration for the Liberty server.

When the project is generated, a `liberty-archetype-webapp/pom.xml` file is also created. This file contains `liberty-maven-plugin`, which is used for packaging, deploying, and running the application on Open Liberty. For further details about the Liberty Maven plugin, visit its home page in the MVNRepository at `https://mvnrepository.com/artifact/io.openliberty.tools/liberty-maven-plugin` and its project page on GitHub at `https://github.com/OpenLiberty/ci.maven`.

The `liberty-archetype-webapp` archetype also includes a sample Java class (`HelloWorldServlet.java`) and a `web.xml` file configuring the servlet.

Notice that `liberty-maven-plugin` is added to your project's `pom.xml` file. The `liberty-maven-plugin` will download and install the Open Liberty runtime, start and stop the server, and deploy your application to the server. It will use the Liberty runtime, which is designed for developing and deploying Java applications in the cloud.

```
<build>
    <!-- Define and configure plugins -->
    <pluginManagement>
        <plugins>
...
...
        <plugin>
            <groupId>io.openliberty.tools</groupId>
            <artifactId>liberty-maven-plugin</artifactId>
            <version>3.6.1</version>
        </plugin>
        </plugins>
    </pluginManagement>
</build>
```

You should also update the following dependencies in your `pom.xml` file to use the latest version of Servlet.

```
<dependency>
    <groupId>jakarta.servlet</groupId>
    <artifactId>jakarta.servlet-api</artifactId>
    <version>5.0.0</version>
</dependency>
```

Now you can start working on your project; you can import the project into your IDE. Run the application on the Liberty server.

```
$ mvn liberty:dev
```

When you make changes to the code, you'll see them automatically reflected in the running server. Table B-1 lists the Maven commands for an Open Liberty server.

Table B-1. *Maven Commands for an Open Liberty Server*

Maven Command	Description
mvn liberty:dev	Downloads, installs, and starts the Open Liberty server for development purposes. It listens for any changes in the project's source code and server configuration. This is very convenient for development, since the server is automatically reloaded and the application is redeployed whenever a change is saved.
mvn liberty:devc	Builds a Docker image, mounts the required directories, maps the required ports, and then runs the application in dev mode in a Docker container. It will also listen to changes to the source code and configuration like dev mode. Based on these changes, the source code is automatically rebuilt, the server is restarted, or the configuration is reloaded, as required.
mvn liberty:create	Creates a new Open Liberty project with a default server.xml file.
mvn liberty:package	Creates a .war file that can be deployed to any Open Liberty server. If it's used with the -Dinclude=runnable option, the command will create a runnable .JAR file with all the required dependencies. This file can then be executed using the java -jar command to start the application.

(continued)

Table B-1. (*continued*)

Maven Command	Description
mvn liberty:deploy	Deploys the application to the running server.
mvn liberty:install-feature	Installs a feature in the local Open Liberty runtime.
mvn liberty:reload	Reloads the server and applications with the latest changes.
mvn liberty:run	First downloads and installs an Open Liberty server runtime to the `target/liberty/wlp` directory in the project, then creates a server instance with the required configuration in the `target/liberty/wlp/usr/servers/defaultServer` directory. It builds and deploy the project to the Open Liberty server using loose config. Finally, it runs the Open Liberty server in the foreground. The loose config feature allows you to change the configuration of your Liberty server without having to redeploy your application. This can be useful for testing different configurations or for troubleshooting problems.
mvn liberty:start	Starts the Open Liberty server in the background.
mvn liberty:stop	Stops the Open Liberty server in the background.
liberty:undeploy	Undeploys an application from the Open Liberty server.

APPENDIX C

Installing Open Liberty Tools

To install the Open Liberty Tools, follow these steps:

1. You must install an Eclipse IDE for Enterprise Java and Web
   Developers (`https://www.eclipse.org/downloads/packages/`
   `release/2022-06/r/eclipse-ide-enterprise-java-and-`
   `web-developers`). Make sure you download the package that
   corresponds to your OS. See Figure C-1.

© Tarun Telang 2023

T. Telang, *Beginning Cloud Native Development with MicroProfile, Jakarta EE, and Kubernetes*,
https://doi.org/10.1007/978-1-4842-8832-0

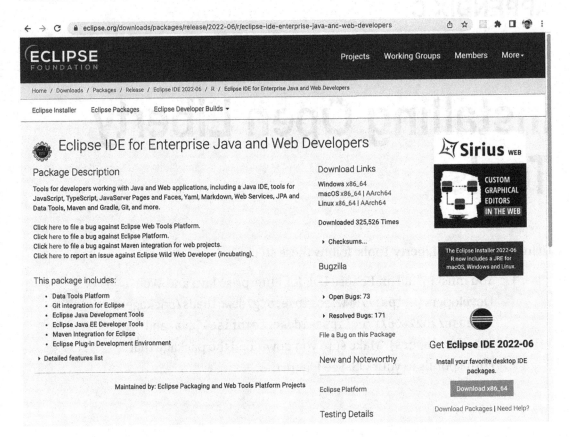

Figure C-1. *Download site for Eclipse IDE for Enterprise Java and Web Developers*

2. Download the .ZIP file of Eclipse Developer Tools to a directory
   of your choice on your computer. It is available at `https://`
   `openliberty.io/start/#eclipse_developer_tools`. See
   Figure C-2.

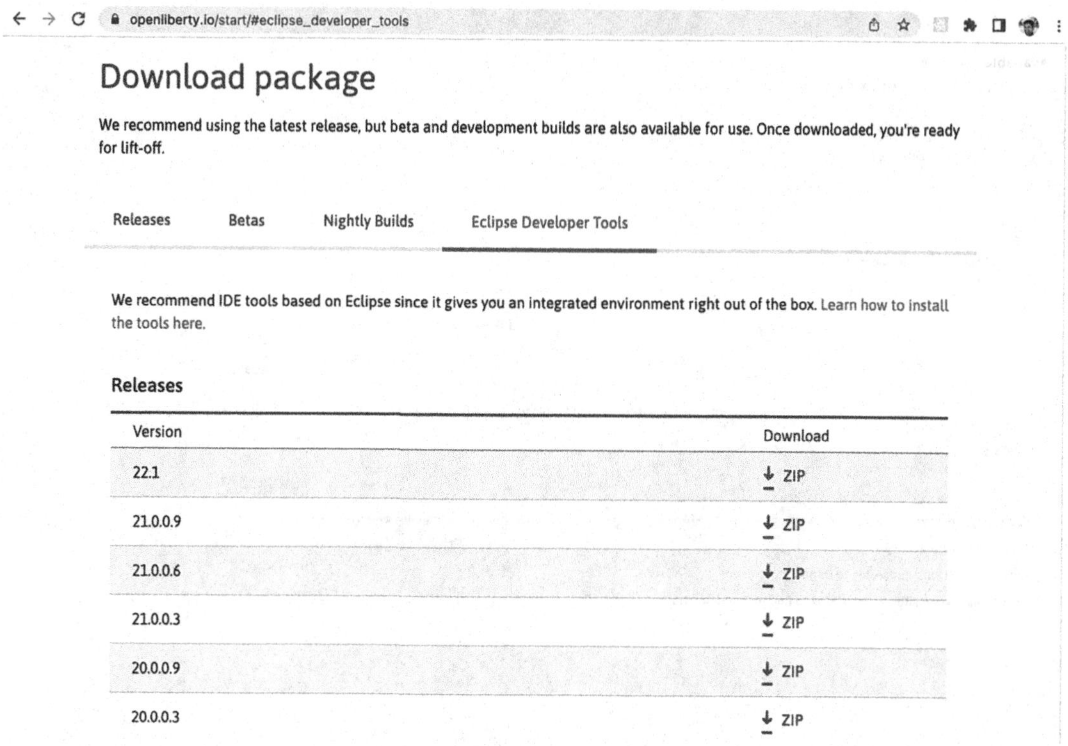

Figure C-2. *Download site for Open Liberty Eclipse Developer Tools*

3. Launch your Eclipse IDE and choose Help ➤ Install New Software ➤ Add.

4. In the Add Repository window, click Archive. See Figure C-3.

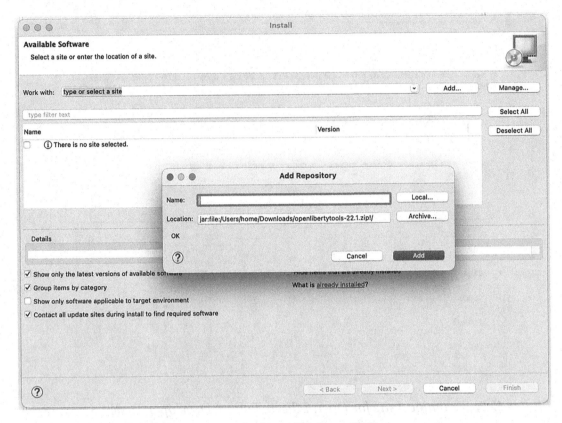

Figure C-3. *The Add Repository window of Eclipse IDE*

5. Browse to the location of the .ZIP file you downloaded in Step 2.
    Select the file and then click Open.

6. Follow the installation instructions on the installation wizard. See
    Figure C-4.

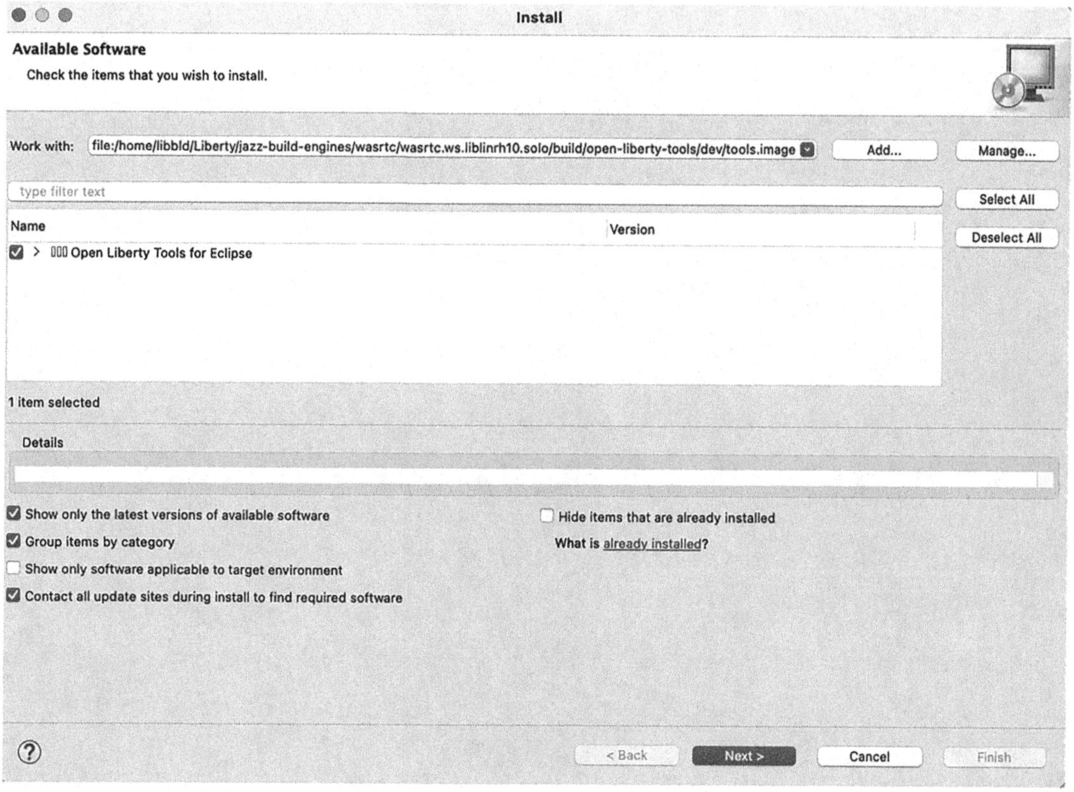

Figure C-4. *Installation wizard of Eclipse IDE*

7.   Once the installation process completes, restart the workbench.

You have successfully installed the Open Liberty Tools on your machine.

Index

A

Active Directory Federation Services (ADFS), 185
Amazon Elastic Container Service (ECS), 39
Amazon Web Services (AWS), 23, 38, 43, 129, 132, 144
Annotation-based approach, 178
@APIResponse annotation, 179
applicationManager element, 94
@ApplicationPath annotation, 176
Application programming interface (API), 46, 77, 148, 171, 177–180, 193, 203, 208–211, 216
Artificial intelligence (AI), 115

B

Bare-metal clusters, 218
Bare-metal hypervisors, 127
Blue-green deployment strategy, 140

C

call() method, 157, 158
Central processing unit (CPU), 127
@Claim annotation, 196
Client-server architecture, 113, 114
Cloud computing
    application types, 4
    benefits, 1, 2, 4, 5
    characteristics, 5–7
    definition, 1
    end-users access, 1
    examples, 2, 3
    HTTP, 21
    Java, 19–21
    services (*see* Service models)
    types, deployment models, 8
        community cloud, 9, 10
        hybrid cloud, 12, 13
        private cloud, 11
        public cloud, 8, 9
    web-based applications, 21
    web services, 22, 23, 26, 27
Cloud-native application
    benefits, 33
    characteristics, 30–32
    definition, 29
    design, 29, 30
    development, 37
    drawbacks, 34
    examples, 32, 33
    vs. traditional applications, 35–37
Cloud Native Computing Foundation (CNCF), 26
ConfigProperty annotation, 150
@Consumes annotation, 105, 107, 206
Container-based application, 26, 128–129, 134–138
Containerization, 37, 46, 53, 54, 65, 124, 228

T. Telang, *Beginning Cloud Native Development with MicroProfile, Jakarta EE, and Kubernetes*, https://doi.org/10.1007/978-1-4842-8832-0

Printed in the United States
by Baker & Taylor Publisher Services